ELOHIM · JEHOVAH · ADONAI · JEHOVAH JIREH · JEHOVAH TSABA · JEHOVAH SHALOM · JEHOVAH ROHI · JEHOVAH NISSI · JEHOVAH MEKKODISHKEM · JEHOVAH RAPHA · JEHOVAH TSIDKENU · EL ELYON · EL SHADDAI · IMMANUEL

EXPERIENCE
THE **POWER** OF
GOD'S NAMES

STRONG CREATOR GOD · THE RELATIONAL GOD · THE GOD WHO RULES · THE LORD WILL PROVIDE · THE LORD OF THE WARRIOR · THE LORD IS ABLE · THE LORD MY SHEPHERD · THE LORD MY BANNER · THE LORD WHO SANCTIFIES · THE LORD WHO HEALS · THE LORD MY RIGHTEOUSNESS · THE MOST HIGH GOD · THE LORD ALMIGHTY · GOD WITH US

TONY EVANS

HARVEST HOUSE PUBLISHERS
EUGENE, OREGON

Interior and cover design by Dugan Design Group

EXPERIENCE THE POWER OF GOD'S NAMES

Copyright © 2017 Tony Evans
Published by Harvest House Publishers
Eugene, Oregon 97402
www.harvesthousepublishers.com

ISBN 978-0-7369-7149-2 (hardcover)
ISBN 978-0-7369-7150-8 (eBook)

Library of Congress Cataloging-in-Publication Data

Names: Evans, Tony, 1949- author.
Title: Experience the power of God's names / Tony Evans.
Description: Eugene, Oregon : Harvest House Publishers, 2017. | Description
  based on print version record and CIP data provided by publisher; resource
  not viewed.
Identifiers: LCCN 2017010309 (print) | LCCN 2017015670 (ebook) | ISBN
  9780736971508 (ebook) | ISBN 9780736971492 (hardcover)
Subjects: LCSH: God (Christianity)--Name--Meditations.
Classification: LCC BT180.N2 (ebook) | LCC BT180.N2 E928 2017 (print) | DDC
  231—dc23
LC record available at https://lccn.loc.gov/2017010309

Printed in the United States of America

17 18 19 20 21 22 23 24 25 / ML / 10 9 8 7 6 5 4 3 2 1

INTRODUCTION

When you pray to God, you probably use several different forms of His name—Lord, Father, Jesus, Creator. Each name conveys certain attributes of God, and your prayers reflect those characteristics. Yet God reveals Himself to us even more than the same three or four names we tend to use in our communion with Him.

The Bible includes more than 85 names of God—each offering us a further glimpse of who God is, what He can do in our world and in our lives, and how He relates to those He created. When we dig a little deeper into the meaning of those names, we grow closer to God as He reveals aspects of Himself to us.

When we call on God by name, He meets our needs. We can ask Him for peace and deliverance from seemingly hopeless circumstances. We can call upon His power to bring productivity and victory into our lives. We can turn to Him when we seek safety and protection. When we speak His name, we experience His encouragement, love, and compassion.

Through the pages of this devotional, you will spend a season immersed in the wondrous names of God. Challenge your heart and your mind to reach new depths in discovering what the Lord wishes for your life. Some of the names might be familiar. Many will be new. Some of the attributes will be expected. Others will be unexpected. But when you consider them prayerfully and ask God to guide your discovery, all will fill your soul with gladness and your heart with praise. Through His mighty name, God's power and might will be made manifest in your life.

ELOHIM
THE STRONG CREATOR GOD

YOU PUT THE UNIVERSE TOGETHER WITH YOUR WORDS. THANK YOU FOR KNOWING HOW >TO PUT MY LIFE TOGETHER AS WELL.

Imagine attempting to build a house or prepare a meal or fix a car with no materials or ingredients or directions. It would be impossible, wouldn't it? You need some basic essentials in order to create. God, however, was able to speak the world into existence with nothing at all—no raw materials, no blueprint, no guidance. He relied only upon His own creative prowess and ingenuity.

We first meet the God of the Bible as *Elohim*, the strong Creator God. And when we reflect upon the vastness of the oceans, the magnitude of the mountain ranges, and the intricacies of the tiniest insects, we are astounded by His masterful work.

In your own life, you can rest secure in the strength of *Elohim*. You don't need to immediately find solutions to all your problems and issues or completely figure out all your plans. You have been created with your own unique passions, skills, and interests, but God is the One who ultimately puts all these things together if you simply live a life directed by Him.

Elohim, the Creator of all things, also knows all things. Filled with wisdom and wonder, He masterfully weaves our life stories. Our job is to listen to Him, seek Him, and live out the story He has planned for us.

Worthy are You, our Lord and our God, to receive glory and honor and power; for You created all things, and because of Your will they existed, and were created.

Revelation 4:11

JEHOVAH
THE RELATIONAL GOD

YOU RULE OVER ALL,
YET YOU ALSO SEEK A

Relationship

WITH YOUR CREATION.

YOU ARE WORTHY OF ALL

*Praise
& Worship.*

When we contemplate the complexity of creation, it can be tempting to think of God as impersonal and uninvolved, a faraway being who set the world spinning but has no personal connection to our lives. Fortunately, the Bible tells us that's far from the truth.

It's true that God is the strong Creator, the one who made heaven and earth. But God is also highly relational—more than anything, He seeks a relationship with His creation. He desires to know us on a personal level. He wishes to walk with us. He yearns to bless us and bring us joy with His presence.

If you're having trouble connecting with God and seeing His hand at work in your life, it might be time to open your eyes and start noticing. Look for the love He pours out—a word of encouragement when you most need it, an answered prayer, grace and patience in the midst of tension and conflict, moments of light in the darkness.

God makes Himself known to us as *Jehovah*—the relational God. He desires to know us fully and, in turn, desires for us to know Him. When we begin to think of the Lord in this manner, we draw closer to Him, abide with Him, and allow His life to direct our steps.

> In this is love, not that we loved God, but that He loved us.
>
> 1 John 4:10

Thank YOU for
Being My LORD
& My MASTER
ADONAI
MASTER OVER ALL
& Yet Allowing
Me to KNOW
YOU Intimately

Laws and rules exist in our world for our own good. Traffic laws are designed to keep us safe when we're traveling down streets and highways. We follow rules and regulations in our homes and offices so we can get along, be productive, and create the healthiest environment possible for living and working. Everything works best when people agree to follow a set of standards that make sense.

Most of all, we need to follow the standards of God. When we submit to His lordship and agree that His guidelines and instructions produce growth in our lives and in our hearts, we live out the plan He has established for us. He is *Adonai*, master over all, and we must obey and follow Him.

But even law-abiding citizens stumble every now and then. You lose track of a speed limit and drive too fast. You forget to return your library books on time. You're stressed out and frustrated, and you forget to treat others the way you'd like to be treated. It happens. And there are consequences to your actions—a speeding ticket, library fines, a fractured friendship.

Submission can be hard. But keep at it. Continue to worship the Lord your God and follow His ways. Look to Him for leading. Submit to His standards. And marvel at His mighty power. He leads, you follow. And He leads you into a place of rejoicing and peace.

I said to the LORD, "You are my Master! Every good thing I have comes from you."

Psalm 16:2 NLT

LIVE IN ME.

EL BETHEL

THE GOD OF THE HOUSE OF GOD

Set Up Your Home
IN THE DEPTHS OF MY SOUL,

AND LET YOUR WORDS

ABIDE IN ME

When you're moving into a brand-new home or setting up a temporary campsite, one of the first things you do is make the space your own. You paint the interior or exterior of the new house and move in your familiar furniture. You pitch your tent in a level spot at the campsite and set your camping chairs around the fire pit. You've claimed the space, whether for a few decades or a few days. It's yours.

God also longs to claim His space—in the depth of our souls. His name *El Bethel* means "the God of the house of God," and the word bethel means "where You dwell." When God takes up residence in us, our bodies are His temples. And because of this, our aim should be to glorify the Lord in all that we do.

Having God take up residence in our lives is the most exciting thing ever, for He can do all things. No purpose of His can ever be thwarted. No plan of His can ever be overcome. His power is all-encompassing and everlasting. The more space you allow Him in your life, the more He will make Himself known to you. Through His gentle guidance, you'll be able to discern what is best, and you'll be able to reflect God well and glorify Him in all things.

Do you not know that you are a temple of God and that the Spirit of God dwells in you?

1 Corinthians 3:16

FROM EVERLASTING TO EVERLASTING,

ELOHE CHASEDDI

GOD OF MERCY

Your Love

IS WITH THOSE WHO HONOR YOU

Life doesn't always guarantee us second chances. There are times when our poor decisions—harsh words spoken to a friend, mistakes made on the job, life choices that aren't healthy—cost us. We lose the friendship. We're dismissed from our job. Our health suffers. Even if we have a change of heart, there's no assurance that everything will be okay.

God's mercy, though, gives us second chance after second chance. *Elohe Chaseddi*—God of mercy—showers us with forgiveness and bathes us with lovingkindness. He is always truthful. Always merciful. Always compassionate. If we love Him and ask Him for His forgiveness, He grants it. Always.

Because He is a God of mercy, we can live unafraid. We always have access to the peace of mind and heart that He so freely gives in abundance. He promises to always be with us and to bring us through every troubling situation and every difficult season. Even when the mistakes are of our own doing, He is forever willing to offer forgiveness to a repentant heart.

Instead of worrying about yesterday, God wants us to focus on today. How can we serve Him today? What plans does He have for us to accomplish today? How can we share Him with others today? That's the beauty of mercy—second chances, looking ahead, with a focus on the future He has for us.

Therefore let us draw near with confidence to the throne of grace, so that we may receive mercy and find grace to help in time of need.

Hebrews 4:16

13

I *Marvel* at the WAY YOU HAVE USED ISRAEL EL ELOHE YISRAEL THE MIGHTY GOD OF ISRAEL to Accomplish YOUR Plan from ETERNITY PAST.

Take a glance at the headlines of today's news. It's difficult to imagine God's peace and promises in the midst of political turmoil and human suffering. It's nearly impossible to find love and grace in the midst of chaos and despair. But even in our troubled world, we need to keep praising the Lord for His plan of salvation and offering Him thanksgiving for His deliverance of us.

Just as God has chosen the nation of Israel as His own, He has also chosen us as individuals. We can read through the story of the Israelite people in the Bible and see how God brought them back to Him time and time again. The story of the nation of Israel mirrors our own stories. Again and again, we stray from God's love. Again and again, He draws us back in.

Even though current circumstances may not look like it, God has granted peace to our world. And He has granted peace to each one of us. We can be the hands and feet of His compassion and mercy. We can speak His words in prayer for the areas of the globe that are being torn apart by conflict. And we can partner with Him in making known to all the saving knowledge of the everlasting God.

Peace I leave with you; My peace I give to you; not as the world gives do I give to you. Do not let your heart be troubled, nor let it be fearful.

John 14:27

EL ELOHIM JEHOVAH

THE MIGHTY ONE, GOD, THE LORD

YOU are stronger than all and everything combined

I PRAISE You for Your power, strength, and might.

Maybe you're having a banner year with your working out, Bible reading, or professional life. But it's pretty rare to be in a place where you're always going strong—physically, emotionally, *and* spiritually. It's impossible to have a perfectly balanced life all the time. And it's also impossible to know *how* to keep a good balance in life, knowing exactly what to do and when to do it. Maybe God wants us invested in something for a season while we're ready to move on to something else. Or He wants us to persevere when we want to give up. He knows the strength we can gain through the struggle.

We aren't always strong, but God is always mighty. He knows all. He is over all. And He is stronger than all and everything combined. That's why it's so important for us to look to Him and draw from His power, strength, and might. We need to recognize our own weaknesses and rest in the power of God instead of attempting to do it all ourselves.

It's easy for us to try to assess our own situations and place our own desires above the things God desires for us. But that's not God's plan. God is mighty enough to accomplish His plan without our help, but because He loves us so much, He gives us a role in the plan.

While you're contemplating God's might, also contemplate His love. It's a healthy love. An unconditional love. And a mighty love.

He gives strength to the weary, and to him who lacks might, He increases power.

Isaiah 40:29

EL ELYON

THE MOST HIGH GOD

YOU HAVE THE POWER TO SAVE. I WILL NOT FEAR WHAT MAN CAN DO BECAUSE YOU ARE THE MOST HIGH GOD.

What happens when you're experiencing that moment you thought you'd never experience? When you wonder if you're being pushed beyond where you thought you could go? When you're not sure if you're ever going to be the same again—and if you even want to keep going on?

Every journey has its share of harrowing moments, and our lives are no exception. Sooner or later, we all reach a point where we wonder if we can take any more. We're overcome with anxiety. Worry has taken up permanent residence in our heart. And fear stifles every other emotion. We're not in control, that's for sure. And, truth be told, we're having a hard time seeing through the fog as we search for God's guidance.

It may seem like the worst advice in the world at a time when you need to take action and find a way out of the mess your life has become, but God tells us to *wait*. He wants us to wait on Him, *El Elyon*, the Most High God. He wants us to stop and look to Him in our times of deepest trouble.

God never faints or grows weary. When we feel faint, He gives us power. When we are weak, He increases our strength. He reaches out His mighty hand to take our anxiety, our worry, our fear. His protection is the promise of the Most High God.

You alone, whose name is the LORD, are the Most High over all the earth.

Psalm 83:18

Neither death nor life, neither fear nor worry...

ELEMUNAH

THE FAITHFUL GOD

NOTHING can separate me from You because You are FAITHFUL.

We like to think we're faithful people. We get to work on time (well, usually) and do our job with diligence. We make time for family and friends. We're involved in our church and sign up for committees and volunteer opportunities. But no matter how hard we try to be faithful, we're not perfect. Inevitably, we're going to miss a meeting or skip a child's soccer game or forget about that volunteer assignment.

Because we can't always be faithful people, it's reassuring to know that we serve a faithful God. His name *El Emunah* means "the faithful God," and He can always be counted on to show up, roll up His sleeves, and get to work in our lives. Always keeps His promises? Check. Always hears our prayers? Check. Always remains with us? Check.

Things happen in our lives that keep us from being totally faithful to others. Because we're human, we're tempted to make choices based on our own self-preservation, selfishness, and greed. Quite simply, we can't be perfect all the time. But when we don't show up, God does. And He gently guides us back to the work He has especially for us to do—the work of being faithful and showing up for others. When we turn to His perfection in our times of imperfection, His faithfulness transforms us.

Your loving-kindness, O LORD, extends to the heavens, Your faithfulness reaches to the skies.

Psalm 36:5

21

I CAN DO NOTHING APART from YOU, SO YOU ARE WORTHY OF all my Heartfelt & Truest Praise.

ELOHEI TEHILLATI

GOD OF MY PRAISE

When you hear the word "praise," what comes to mind? Your favorite worship song? A sermon you recently heard about glorifying God? An inspirational book you read about giving the Lord our praise and worship?

It can be tempting to think of praise as a Sunday-only thing, or something we do as part of our morning devotional time or evening prayer. And while God does desire that we worship Him on a regular basis, which can often be scheduled into our busy lives, we need to remember that praise is a lifestyle for the believer.

Start seeing your life from a spiritual perspective. We all have moments when we do something right or something goes our way and we try to take credit for what God has done. But remember, we can't do anything apart from God. He's the one who ultimately deserves gratitude and glory in every aspect of our lives.

God is our strength and our song—on Sunday morning, during our devotional time, and in every other part of our lives. He deserves glory for all good things, and He deserves our worship all week long. So look for opportunities to praise Him when you're taking your daily walk, doing that dreaded task at work...even when you're grocery shopping. The miracle of His love often shows up in the most unexpected places when we live a lifestyle of praise.

> **Through Him then, let us continually offer up a sacrifice of praise to God, that is, the fruit of lips that give thanks to His name.**
>
> Hebrews 13:15

23

BECAUSE OF *Jesus,*

I AM ABLE TO COME INTO YOUR PRESENCE WITH UNVEILED FACE AND BEHOLD THE GLORY OF THE LORD.

EL HAKABODH

GOD OF GLORY

When you're in the presence of someone you admire—an amazing athlete, an inspirational speaker, a talented musician—you're captivated by that individual. You watch their every move, pay attention to their every word, listen to their every note. You wouldn't think of opening a book or scrolling through social media on your phone or becoming bored and walking away. You want to soak up that person's presence for as long as you can!

Through His creation, His works, His Word, and His Spirit, God shows us that more than any other, He is worthy of our admiration. He is *El Hakabodh*, God of glory, and we should be captivated by His presence above all others. When He's trying to get our attention, we should never turn away.

One of the many amazing aspects of Jesus's life is the fact that the Son made it possible for us to see the Father. And when we truly see God for who He is, we should never feel the need to turn away. His compassion, His love, His generosity, His steadfastness—we'll never run out of words that attest to His attributes and His accomplishments. The more we know Him, the more magnificent we will realize His glory to be. And the more we will long to remain in the presence of our glorious Lord and Savior.

Worthy are You, our LORD and our God, to receive glory and honor and power; for You created all things, and because of Your will they existed, and were created.

Revelation 4:11

All that is *living*—
every
ANIMAL, CELL, FLOWER, HUMAN BEING...
every living thing
receives
its life
from
Your own.

ELOHIM
CHAYIM
THE LIVING GOD

If you're an outdoorsy person and enjoy camping, fishing, or hiking, you've experienced firsthand the wonder of God's creative power and the amazing array of living things He has made. Even if your outdoorsy bent is limited to front-porch flower gardening and caring for your pets, you still nurture an appreciation for *Elohim Chayim*—the living God—who is the source of all life.

When you take this appreciation for God's creative power one step further, you experience God's involvement in the entirety of your life. When you allow Him access to your heart, you welcome His presence in everything you do. The decisions you make, the words you speak, the goals you strive to achieve—all are based on the living God.

The God who created the universe wants nothing more than to form you, guide you, and challenge you as you become all He intended you to be. His greatest wish is to be a loving participant in your life.

Imagine—the living God has an overwhelming interest in you and your life. It's almost unbelievable, but it's true. He cares about you. He is concerned about you. He isn't distant and removed from you. He walks with you and goes before you and is completely alive and active in your present life, ready to help you settle into the destiny He has planned for you.

Then the LORD God formed man of dust from the ground, and breathed into his nostrils the breath of life; and man became a living being.

Genesis 2:7

EL HAYYAY

THE GOD OF MY LIFE

YOU ARE THE GOD OF MY LIFE. YOU DIRECT MY STEPS ACCORDING TO YOUR WILL AND DESIRE. YOU CAUSE ME *to walk on firm footing.*

If you've ever walked from total darkness into bright light, you probably had a hard time seeing right away. Your eyes had become so accustomed to the darkness that the light blinded you, and you couldn't make out the images right in front of you.

Walking without God is like making our way through life in total darkness. We grasp at anything we can get our hands on, desperate to make our way to a place where we can recognize anything at all. Every bit of patience leaves us, and we become impetuous, making poor decisions and stumbling our way through circumstances, losing all sense of direction.

Those are the times when we need to stop and turn to the light God provides. If you really want to know how things are going to turn out, dive into His Word. Seek His presence through prayer. Open your ears to Him and soften your heart to discern His Spirit. Recognize when He wants to lead you in a new direction and place your feet on a different path.

Life may take us by surprise, but nothing happens to us that is a surprise to God. Everything has first passed through His capable hands. He is *El Hayyay*, the God of our lives. And He brings us into the light when we determine to seek His way.

The Light shines in the darkness, and the darkness did not comprehend it.

John 1:5

ELOHIM KEDOSHIM

THE HOLY GOD

I Praise You

AS THE LORD

My God,

AND I CONSECRATE MYSELF BEFORE YOU TO BE HOLY AS YOU ARE HOLY.

Have you ever had a day when absolutely everything went right? Everything? Even if you have a day when you get pretty close, there's no such thing as perfection in this fallen world. And while God desires for us to aim for holiness, He knows that we'll always fall short.

God dwells in a high and holy place, but He also hangs out with those who have contrite and humble hearts. When we confess our own imperfection and open the door to His work in our lives, God's holiness cleanses us. He wipes away the stain of our sin. And He makes us more like Him.

Our goal in life should be to reflect God's glory and goodness. When others look at us, they need not see perfection. They should instead see someone who relies on God's grace and love. When our hearts are filled with worry, doubt, fear, anxiety, anger, and a host of other unpleasant emotions, we need to give those feelings to God and ask Him to show us favor and patience. Before we even begin to make a wrong choice or think a wrong thought, we need to invite God into our hearts and minds and ask Him to speak to us. It's a process, to be sure, and not always an easy one. But little by little, we can seek His heart and do our best to live a life that reflects the goodness of our holy God.

There is no one holy like the LORD, indeed, there is no one besides You, nor is there any rock like our God.

1 Samuel 2:2

EL KANNA,
THE JEALOUS GOD

If You didn't love me

MORE DEEPLY
THAN I CAN EVEN
UNDERSTAND

You would not be jealous.

When you're faced with a pressing dilemma or a tough decision, the natural response is to ask a trusted friend or mentor for advice. And while this can be an important primary step, the *very* first thing you should do is seek God's presence and wisdom. Ask Him, "Lord, please give me the spiritual discernment to know what to do. Please make Your plan clear to me and show me Your hand at work it this situation."

Our goal in life is to be holy as God is holy, and that's why we need to turn to Him before we seek help anywhere else. After we've gone to God with an open and humble heart, He may very well direct us to seek advice from that trusted friend. But the difference is that we'll be more inclined to listen to that guidance with a spirit of discernment. We'll be able to better see God's direction and assess what is clearly from Him.

God takes the name of *El Kanna*, the jealous God, because He deserves to be first in our lives. Indeed, when we disregard His Word or take someone else's advice instead of His, it pains God. He loves us that much. And so we should always turn to Him first, with the goal of living a life of holiness that truly respects God and blesses others.

He jealously longs for the spirit he has caused to dwell in us.

James 4:5 NIV

GIVE ME YOUR GREAT STRENGTH

ELOHEI MA'UZZI

THE GOD OF MY STRENGTH

SO I CAN WITHSTAND TEMPTATION AND DO ALL YOU HAVE ASSIGNED ME TO DO.

W e're used to doing things for ourselves. We admire the DIY mindset, in which individuals take it upon themselves to create or fix anything and everything. And while this self-sufficiency is admirable in many ways, we shouldn't take a DIY approach to *all* aspects of our lives.

Sometimes it's imperative that we look to each other for help, and beyond that, we need to look to God. He created the earth—the ultimate DIY. And He continues to create anew. His creation testifies to His power and strength, and we need to remember this during those stubborn times when we're determined to walk in our own limited power. He is *Elohei Ma'uzzi*, the God of our strength, and we need Him.

Go ahead and breathe a big sigh of relief. You're not a failure if you don't DIY it all. You don't have to juggle everything on your own. No matter what you're struggling with, no matter what temptations you face, God is there to bring you through and strengthen your resolve.

Don't be afraid to dream big and have big plans. We *need* to think big because we serve a big God. But if we aim for big things and don't look to the Lord for help, we're destined to fail big. Instead, we need to rely on God's incredible strength and access it on a regular basis. When we do this, we live out our destiny.

But You, LORD, do not be far from me; you are my strength; come quickly to help me.

Psalm 22:19 NIV

I adore
You because
ELOHIM
MACHASE LANU
GOD OUR REFUGE
You provide
A PLACE
where I can
go when the
STORMS OF LIFE
toss me here
and there.

When you're caught in a storm, is your first instinct to take on the tempest by yourself? Do you head outside to meet the tornado or hurricane or blizzard face-to-face? Not a chance! You look for the safest place you can, preferably in the company of close family or friends. Nobody likes to be alone in a storm, and nobody wants to wait out the squall without shelter.

The storms of life toss us here and there, and we all have our own means of fighting them. We look for distractions. We seek out others. Sometimes we even look the other way and pretend nothing is happening. But that's not the shelter-in-place plan God has created for us.

God promises to keep us safe with Him in the midst of trouble. When we're feeling vulnerable or out of control or completely confused, He provides a place for us to go. He is *Elohim Machase Lanu*, God our refuge, and He takes care of us when we seek out His protection.

Like a substantial storm shelter, God is great and mighty. Nothing can penetrate His strength. But at the same time, His care for us is gentle and protective. He washes away our worry, and fear fades in His presence. When the storms of life hit, we may falter, but if we lean on God, we will not fall.

God is our refuge and strength, a very present help in trouble.

Psalm 46:1

37

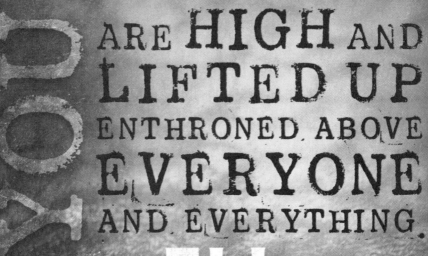

YOU ARE HIGH AND LIFTED UP ENTHRONED ABOVE EVERYONE AND EVERYTHING.

ELI MAELEKHI

GOD MY KING

I HUMBLY OFFER YOU MY PRAISE.

What reigns as king of your life? If you're uncertain of your answer, reflect on how you spent the past day or two. Were you methodically checking off the boxes on your own to-do list, or did you leave room for God in the midst of your many commitments?

Now, I'm not saying you should ditch the agenda or erase everything from your calendar. Responsibilities are important, and we honor God when we work with diligence and dedication. But when we put our own plans above God's kingdom agenda, that's when the problem arises. We are heirs to His kingdom and children of the King, and we must take our role seriously.

When we pray, "Your kingdom come" and "Your will be done," we should meditate on what those words truly mean. Having a kingdom mindset means using God's Word as our guide in every decision we make and in every interaction we have with others. We need to immerse ourselves in the Lord's way of thinking so we know what He would have us do and say in every situation.

As we would honor a king, we should give God our praise, adoration, and commitment. When we find ourselves slipping away from His guidance, we need to eliminate the distractions in our life and listen for His voice. We need to truly make Him King in our lives.

> Seek first His kingdom and His righteousness, and all these things will be added to you.
>
> Matthew 6:33

You are the
RADIANCE *of*
GOD'S GLORY
and the EXACT
REPRESENTATION
of Him in every way.
HUIOS
TOU THEOU
THE SON OF GOD
I lift up Your name.

One of the many names of God that should have extra special meaning for us is *Huios Tou Theou*. Not familiar with it? That's understandable. Translated, it means the Son of God. Otherwise known as Jesus.

Jesus is the Son of God, but He is also indeed the very picture of the heavenly Father. The familiar phrase "Like father, like son" couldn't be more true in this instance. Jesus radiates God's glory and is the exact representation of Him in every way. And because of His death, burial, and resurrection, we're able to receive forgiveness for all we've done and to be born anew.

We need to keep our connection with Jesus tight. We need to honor Him with every part of our lives and keep Him close in all we do. As we rest in Him and discover more about His love, we'll learn to live out His will and His way.

The best way to keep close to Jesus is to get to know His words. Read them over and over in Scripture. Meditate on their meaning. Put yourself in His position, walking and talking with the disciples and communing with the Father. Observe how He treats others. Notice how His heart responds. And then strive to be like Him in all that you do.

God so loved the world, that He gave His only begotten Son, that whoever believes in Him shall not perish, but have eternal life.

John 3:16

EL NEKAMOTH

THE GOD WHO AVENGES

YOU INVITE ME
TO YOUR TABLE
WHEN OTHERS
OPPOSE ME.
YOU SET ME IN
HIGH PLACES
WHEN THEY TRY TO
TAKE ME DOWN.

Revenge plays a big role in today's culture. From world events to personal problems, our first instinct is to right the wrong and get even. Admirers of quick action, we champion swift retaliation and become impatient when, in our opinion, justice is not being served.

God's Word, however, commands us to be slow to anger. God extols the virtues of patience, forgiveness, and compassion—virtues that don't seem to go hand in hand with vengeance. Sometimes we should answer with silence when others oppose us. Sometimes we should turn away when we've been wronged. And sometimes we should act with restraint when we want to dive right in.

Now, this isn't to say that we shouldn't stand up for others or that we should close our eyes to sin. God definitely gives us the green light to take godly action. But we need to make sure that our hearts are aligned with God's will. Sometimes God wants us to stay out of the picture when He's busy balancing the scales of justice. His compassion can right any wrong, and in His love He will always intervene on our behalf and remove, correct, or bring repentance to the person who has treated us unfairly. So remain patient. Stay in control. Wait upon the Lord. Because in the end, He is victorious.

Beloved, never avenge yourselves, but leave it to the wrath of God, for it is written, "Vengeance is mine, I will repay, says the LORD."

Romans 12:19 ESV

EL NOSE

THE GOD WHO FORGIVES

Thank You

FOR THE GRACE
AND MERCY OF
YOUR
FORGIVENESS
IN MY LIFE
*and all it allows me
to experience.*

In a world filled with major wrongdoings, it's easy to ignore the small sins we commit. A flippant comment made to a coworker. A twisting of the truth. A lack of regard for someone else's feelings. These mistakes don't really matter, do they?

Actually, they do matter. Quite a lot. Sin is sin, and all sin needs to be forgiven.

The bottom line is this: God has forgiven us for *all* our sins. And He expects us to acknowledge that in our hearts and minds as we live our lives motivated to serve and honor Him. Now, this doesn't mean you need to keep a notebook with you at all times, marking down your sins and checking off when you've asked for forgiveness. But you do need to have an awareness of your words and thoughts and actions. And you do need to be tuned in to the Lord so He can teach you and guide you.

We don't have to be perfect, but we do need to be persistent in our walk with Jesus, experiencing His love when we ask Him to cleanse us of our sins and rejoicing in His steadfastness and sovereignty. He is *El Nose*, the God who forgives, and because of Him we are able to have abundant life.

> If we confess our sins, He is faithful and righteous to forgive us our sins and to cleanse us from all unrighteousness.
>
> 1 John 1:9

You Are My **God** *Forever & Ever.*

ELOHENU
OLAM

EVERLASTING GOD

YOU WILL BE MY GUIDE
EVEN TO THE END.

Can you imagine what your life will be like five or ten years down the road? You might think you have an idea, but when the future arrives and you glance back five or ten years, you might realize there's no way to predict what the future holds. Life can take unexpected twists and turns. It's unpredictable.

Now attempt to comprehend the existence of God—how He existed before time and how He will never experience an end. How is that remotely possible? While you could do some serious mental gymnastics attempting to explain this, it's comforting to instead rest in His everlasting presence. People in our lives come and go, but God remains constant. Unchanging. Forever and ever.

When you're overwhelmed by the evening news or stressed out at the office or frustrated with your relationships, step back and imagine God holding every problem close to His heart. The universe is like a pebble in His hand, yet He cares about it. All of it. He sees the end before we can even glimpse the beginning. He realizes what we need before we even recognize something is missing. He reads the map of our lives before we've had the chance to unfold them.

Ask God for His wisdom, and He will help you use your time to advance His kingdom for His glory.

But you, O LORD, abide forever, and Your name to all generations.

Psalm 102:12

You
PROVIDE ME
with ALL I NEED
to carry out the
PURPOSE

ELOHIM
OZER LI
GOD MY HELP

for which You have
placed me on earth.

Vacations are the best. You're away from work, away from household chores, away from all the little things that demand your time. Sure, those things aren't going to disappear when the trip is over, but you can temporarily forget they exist. A coworker will pick up the slack at work. A neighbor will take care of your yard and pets. And the weeds in the garden can just grow for a while.

Now, imagine what would happen if God took a vacation. Yikes! On second thought, let's *not* imagine that scenario. We rely on God's help all the time. There's no way to effectively get through a trial or a struggle without Him. The thought of God leaving the planet spinning on its own while He takes a two-week getaway? Let's not even go there!

We can praise God that He never takes a vacation from our lives. He doesn't even take a break when we're sleeping, leaving us completely on our own. He's always there, even when we aren't looking to Him. His help is always available, even when we aren't expecting it. When we make the mistake of turning to our own ways and wisdom, God remains steadfast in our lives, ready to meet us when we turn back to Him. How thankful we are for the kindness of His love, the wisdom of His mind, and the strength of His arm. How grateful we are for His ever-present help.

Trust in the LORD with all your heart and do not lean on your own understanding.

Proverbs 3:5

EL ROI

THE GOD WHO SEES ME

You are not a Distant God, isolated from those You have made. Instead, You see me, You are with me, and You care.

It's human nature to want to be seen. To be recognized for a job well done. To be singled out for possessing a particular skill. To be applauded for victory. Or even just to be noticed. Every one of us longs to be known, and every one of us knows how it feels to be forgotten or ignored. Being seen is important to us.

Sometimes we tend to grumble about God not seeing us. *Does He even care?* we wonder. *Does He have any idea who I am and what I'm going through?* When the world has let us down, it's easy for these wrong thoughts to take possession in our minds. But those thoughts don't tell the truth. The truth is that God *does* see us as individuals. Beyond that, He knows us better than anyone else ever could. After all, He created us.

God sees the whole of our lives—where we've come from and where we're headed. Because He is so attentive to us, He knows just which doors to open and exactly what paths to guide us on. He sees us, and we need to see Him too.

Best of all, God doesn't see us as the world does. He isn't preoccupied with our external appearance. What the world esteems is not of His concern. He sees our hearts, and we will never fade from His mind. That's recognition worth celebrating.

His eyes are upon the ways of a man, and He sees all his steps.

Job 34:21

YOU ARE A FIRM FOUNDATION
I CAN BUILD MY LIFE ON

EL SALI
GOD MY ROCK

YOU PROVIDE MY
Salvation
AND THE STABILITY
OF MY TIMES.

When one of your family members is unhappy, there's a good chance the rest of the family is unhappy too. Our emotions influence others. Anger and sadness and frustration can be contagious. Likewise, happiness and joy can be caught as well. When one person is in a good mood, that upbeat attitude can have a positive effect on others.

God makes Himself known to us as *El Sali*, our rock. Or more like a giant boulder. Unlike us, with our easily caught emotions and moods, He stays steady when everything else crumbles and falls. God does not sway when storms come, and He stands strong when trouble arrives. He is our rock, a firm foundation upon which we would be wise to build our lives.

Isn't it refreshing to know that you have an ever-present source of stability when nothing around you is stable? When the ground around you begins to shake, all you need to do is step onto the ground of His unshakable presence. In the times of unrest—when work or family or health seem shaky and nothing seems solid—the Lord is your rock. Even when we can't see Him or we think we can't feel His presence, He remains steadfast and unwavering. His never-ending kingdom and eternal throne are unmoved because He is our solid rock. When you lean on God, you are made strong. And those who are weak will see your strength and come to know the Father you so willingly serve.

They remembered that God was their rock, and the Most High God their Redeemer.

Psalm 78:35

EL SHADDAI
ALMIGHTY GOD

AS THE
HEAVENS
ARE HIGHER
THAN THE EARTH,
SO YOUR WAYS
REACH HIGHER THAN
MY OWN

Life can be overwhelming. Impossible to understand. Full of unknowns and what-ifs and problems that seem to have no solutions. But through it all, there is one constant, one hope—the Almighty God.

God is always with us—in our struggles and in our blessings. He walks—even runs—beside us on our best days when the sun is shining and everything seems to be working in our favor. And He carries us on our worst days—the days when we're sure the sun has forever disappeared behind the clouds. His power is great and mighty. Nothing is stronger. Nothing is more secure. Nothing can change who He is and what He represents. And nobody will ever love us with a deeper love.

God Almighty is strong in His caring and His compassion. He's also strong in His forgiveness. No matter what we've done or said or thought, He is always ready to forgive us. He understands the dilemmas we're facing and the multitude of unanswered questions we have. In return, He offers us His love, His promises, and His protection.

When you place your trust in *El Shaddai*, the Almighty God of the universe, you place yourself in the most capable hands of all. Stay connected to Him. Rely on His strength. Surround yourself with the blessings of His provision. Hold fast to His promises, and He will always carry you through.

He who dwells in the shelter of the Most High will abide in the shadow of the Almighty.

Psalm 91:1

ELOHIM SHOPHTIM BA-ARETS

THE GOD WHO JUDGES IN THE EARTH

YOUR JUSTICE IS LIKE THE SPRING RAIN, *bringing blessing and life to* THOSE IT TOUCHES.

There are two sides to justice—innocent or guilty. Right or wrong. Good or evil. Among His many other names, God goes by *Elohim Shophtim Ba-arets*, the God who judges in the earth. And God's justice is nothing to mess around with. Our choice is simple—with God or against Him.

If we choose to follow God, we will delight in His justice. It is like a spring rain, bringing blessing and life to those it touches. But if we elect to turn away from the Lord, His justice will bring terror into our lives. He judges both the righteous and the wicked. There will come for all a time of accounting, and God is ultimately in control.

Now, God realizes that our actions aren't always right. Sometimes we do things that offend Him or hurt others or cause turmoil. But He promises to reward those who diligently seek Him. He can see our hearts, and He judges our actions based on what we hold inside us.

When you're distraught by the suffering you see on earth, have hope. As much sadness as you see, as much as your heart hurts, God sees and hurts even more. Rest assured that no evil deed will go unpunished in the end, and every good action will be rewarded. He is the God who judges the earth, and in the end He will bring peace and goodness.

The heavens declare His righteousness, for God Himself is judge.

Psalm 50:6

YOU ARE MY *Delight,*

AND I COME BEFORE YOU IN **PRAYER** TO EXALT YOUR NAME *Forever.*

EL SIMCHATH GILI

GOD MY EXCEEDING JOY

Think about the joy you experience when you master something for the first time. Perhaps you learned a foreign language well enough to finally be able to communicate with native speakers in another country. Or you put in mile after mile and finally crossed the finish line of a marathon. Maybe you've been trying for years to earn your college degree, and you finally step up on that stage to collect your diploma. You feel a plethora of emotions, but joy is always at the forefront.

All good things come from God, and He rejoices in all good things. He is the only and true source of joy, and when we put our trust in Him, we can experience joy in all our circumstances. We can have joy in the midst of struggle if our hope is in the Lord.

The mistake we often make is seeking joy outside of God. When we value ourselves according to someone else's opinion of us or the salary we earn or our social position, we miss out on real joy. We miss the joy in the journey, the joy of discovery, the joy of a heart open to God. And we also miss the incredible opportunity to share the joy of the Lord with others. But when we're filled with the joy that comes from God, we radiate love and pleasure to those around us and know true joy.

Now may the God of hope fill you with all joy and peace in believing, so that you will abound in hope by the power of the Holy Spirit.

Romans 15:13

WHO IS A KING

like YOU,
full of GLORY
and MIGHT,

ELOHIM
TSEBAOTH

GOD OF HOSTS

whose VOICE instructs
those in BATTLE on
behalf of Your children?

When you were a kid, did anyone stand up for you whenever another person was mean to you? Maybe a big brother or sister or a trustworthy friend went to bat for you. Or a parent or teacher helped protect you from harm. You may have fought some battles on your own, but at other times the problem was too big for you to handle alone. That's when you relied on that trusted sibling or friend or adult to step in for backup.

Life is filled with battles. Sometimes we've brought on the problem ourselves, and we need to take action to improve the situation. At other times, we're not at all to blame. Heartbreak, pain, and difficulty seek us out, and we feel unequipped to fight on our own. No matter who or what is to blame, we can always call on *Elohim Tsebaoth*, the God of hosts, to join us in the battle.

In a culture that commands us to take action on our own, we tend to go about our daily business with no regard for others—including God. When we're struggling to overcome our emotions or lamenting that we're being treated unfairly, we keep the focus on ourselves. Instead, we need to allow God to lead the charge and follow His instructions. With God on our side, we will always win the battle.

The LORD is my strength and my shield; my heart trusts in Him, and I am helped; therefore my heart exults, and with my song I shall thank Him.

Psalm 28:7

ELOHE TISHUATHI

GOD OF MY SALVATION

I GIVE YOU PRAISE FOR YOUR POWERFUL HAND & YOUR FORGIVING HEART.

God desires for every one of us to receive the amazing gift of His salvation, and He can bring people to a saving knowledge of Him in many different ways. People can be saved through sermons, teachings, books, and even dreams. But perhaps the best way to come to Christ is when God works through another person.

In a world where so much has gone wrong, it's easy for our hearts to be hardened and for us to lack faith. Used to doing things our own way, we tend to question God's plan—especially when it seems to push us out of our comfort zone. And it's easy to harbor a lack of pure love toward others, especially when we're used to guarding our hearts and protecting ourselves.

But nothing is more important than salvation. That's why it breaks God's heart every time He witnesses us turning away from those in need. He has blessed us so that we might be a blessing to others, and when we choose to keep His love to ourselves, it saddens our Father. We need to remember God as *Elohe Tishuathi*, the God of our salvation, and live each day motivated to serve Him more. We need to search for moments each day to share about His great love and testify to the saving power of His Son, Jesus Christ.

The LORD is my strength and song, and He has become my salvation; this is my God, and I will praise Him.

Exodus 15:2

ELOHE TSADEKI

GOD OF MY RIGHTEOUSNESS

Thank You For making Your

RIGHTEOUSNESS & WISDOM

Available to all through Your Spirit and Your Word.

We're always looking for the next big thing. The secret to becoming organized. The key to getting in shape. The surefire plan to financial stability. We read books, listen to podcasts, and sign up for seminars. And while organization, physical fitness, and financial security are all worthy pursuits, we need to make sure we're not missing the big picture when we're seeking the next big thing.

The main point of life is to follow God, to become like Him and live our lives for Him. And becoming like God means growing in goodness and righteousness. From the Lord flows mercy, grace, might, and strength—all qualities we need in our lives and in our world. God gives us all we need through His Word and Spirit to live in abundant joy. When we choose His desires over our own and strive to become more like Him, He guides and directs us.

Following God's plan may be more challenging than sticking with six easy steps to getting fit or ten ways to cut the clutter in your home. But it's way more rewarding. When we turn to God and hand our lives over to Him, He forgives us and gifts us with His compassion. He helps mend our broken relationships and fills our hearts with righteousness, grace, and peace. Good fruit comes from following God and allowing His righteousness to guide our steps.

Peacemakers who sow in peace reap a harvest of righteousness.

James 3:18 NIV

YOU ARE THE
GOD OF JACOB
& MY GOD,
ELOHE
YAKOB
THE GOD OF JACOB
IN CHRIST
I HAVE BEEN GIVEN
EVERY SPIRITUAL
BLESSING
IN THE
HEAVENLY PLACES.

We're tied to the tangible in this life. If we can see it, smell it, touch it, or taste it, we can prove that something indeed exists. We live in a world of scientific proof, of facts and figures, of the known and experienced. And that's why spirituality is sometimes so challenging to grasp.

It's easy to dismiss the stirrings of God in our spirit when the noise of life is crowding out His voice. But just as God was a personal God to those in the Bible, He remains a personal God to believers today. He is *Elohe Yakob*, the God of Jacob, and we need to recognize His personal attachment in our lives.

Just as He did in the Bible, the Lord hears us in our distress and delivers us time and time again. His name is a name of protection and provision, and He has called and chosen us to walk with Him and help Him advance His kingdom agenda on this earth.

Keep listening for His voice. Continue to search for His guidance. Turn your heart to His heart. And pray daily that He will keep you fully walking in the promises and blessings He has assigned especially for you. His work in your life will be visible proof of His glorious presence.

The righteous cry, and the LORD hears and delivers them out of all their troubles.

Psalm 34:17

THE OCEANS ARE BUT A DROP TO YOU.

ELOHEI MAROM

GOD ON HIGH

The highest peak on earth is Your footstool because You are

GOD ON HIGH.

Our world is fragile. With so much tension and conflict and confusion, it seems like everything is at the breaking point. From relationships between nations to relationships between family members, nothing seems secure. Everything seems unpredictable. We're not quite sure what to expect. Despite the fragility of the world, though, we can take comfort in the assurance that God is holding it all together.

As *Elohei Marom*, God on high, the Lord is to be honored, loved, and adored at all times. He has the power and the ability to heal and solve every problem and issue, no matter how bleak the situation may seem. We can't come close to comprehending the vastness of who God is, but when we glimpse His magnificent creation, we can begin to get some idea of His grandeur.

When everything around you seems like it's about to fall apart, put your trust in the Lord. Recognize Him for who He is—the God of the universe who sits on high—but also thank Him that He is willing to meet us where we're at. Our problems are easily solved by a God who is high and exalted. Nothing surprises Him. Nothing is too difficult for Him to accomplish. Nothing can stand in the way of His eternal plan. If we live our lives according to His will, God will grant us the wisdom to overcome our struggles and find victory in His glorious name and position—*Elohei Marom*, God on high.

You, O LORD, are on high forever.

Psalm 92:8

69

I GIVE YOU
My Gratitude
ELOHEI
HAELOHIM
THE GOD OF GODS
BECAUSE
EVERYTHING
I ENJOY AND
EVERYTHING THAT
HELPS ME GROW
Comes from You.

It's easy to say we don't have idols today. A golden statue that we bow down to? Nope. Don't have one of those. But when we're struggling with the pressures of life, modern-day idols tend to pop up to the surface. If you find yourself obsessed with thoughts about your career, your status, or your relationships, there's a pretty good chance you're dealing with an idol in your life.

When we look to idols, we look away from God. And we miss out on Him drawing us nearer, deepening our relationship with Him. When we follow God in righteousness and truth, He makes our paths straight and guides us into His everlasting love. He is all we need in the moment of darkness—and all we will ever need.

God is stronger, wiser, and higher than anything we can imagine. With Him in control, nothing is impossible. Did you know that He can solve your issues and trials with just a thought or an inclination? It's true. That's why we need to plant His thoughts in our minds and seek His truth above all else.

Every good thing in our lives ultimately comes from Him, so we don't need to look anywhere else for fulfillment or help. Once we've found our place as children of the Lord, we have no need for idols or anything else that clutters the path that leads to His presence.

I love those who love me; and those who diligently seek me will find me.

Proverbs 8:17

Thank You for choosing me to be Your friend.

EHYEH ASHER EHYEH

THE ETERNAL, ALL-SUFFICIENT GOD

Your sufficiency makes me whole.

We can thank God that we can reach out to Him in times of trial and tribulation. But we also need to know that He is with us on days that are quiet and calm. And we need to continue to seek His presence during those times as well.

No matter what season we find ourselves in, we are insufficient in our own power. The Lord, though, is all-sufficient. His power and grace and love are more than enough, and they will sustain us through the valleys and peaks of life. When we're feeling rested and reassured, God is there. And when we're experiencing emotions of restlessness and resentment, He remains by our side.

Even though He's the eternal and limitless God, He chooses to be our faithful friend. And He has given us a heart that longs to be known by Him. The best way to be known by the Lord is to spend time with Him each day and go to Him in prayer. Pray when you're weak and weary. Pray when you're excited and energized. Pray in times of trouble. Pray in times of rejoicing. All the while, remember that God is beyond our capacity of thinking or comprehension—there's no limit to His love or what He can do in our lives. For that we will joyfully thank and praise Him.

"I am the Alpha and the Omega," says the LORD God, "who is and who was and who is to come, the Almighty."

Revelation 1:8

YOU HAVE

CONTROL OVER

All THE EARTH

YOU CREATED.

JEHOVAH

ADON KOL HA-ARETS

THE LORD, THE LORD OF ALL THE EARTH

IT IS YOUR **PLAYGROUND,**

AND IT IS UNDER YOUR COMMAND.

W'e're accustomed to finding prompt solutions to our problems. We want immediate answers, situations that resolve quickly, and speedy results. But that's not always how God works. He is *Jehovah Adon Kol Ha-arets*, the Lord, the Lord of all the earth, and He works in His own ways and in His own timing. Our own finite minds can have difficulty seeing a way through trouble. Indeed, we may sometimes wonder if there *is* a way through, but God can always find a way.

God has control over all He has created. He's not bound by the laws of science or what we may think is possible or even rational. Nothing is too big for God or too removed from His control. Nothing shakes Him. Nothing surprises Him. Nothing catches Him off guard.

Doubting is human nature. If we don't understand how something happened or how something could happen, our first instinct is to doubt it. But that doubt should never apply to God. He is still capable of doing miraculous work, and He still does mighty acts on behalf of His people. It's in His nature. That's why we need to keep our eyes fixed on Jesus—so we can witness the miraculous work He's doing in our lives as well as in the lives of those around us. May our hearts and minds always be open to anything the Lord of all the earth chooses to do in us and through us.

These are just the beginning of all that he does, merely a whisper of his power. Who, then, can comprehend the thunder of his power?

Job 26:14 NLT

YOU are my SHIELD, MY HELPER, & my glorious SWORD.

JEHOVAH CHEREB

THE LORD, THE SWORD

In You alone I find my Victory.

As you work your way through the pages of this devotional, you might be feeling a little overwhelmed by the sheer number of names God goes by. Don't worry—there won't be a test at the end! (And also don't fret if you find some of His names impossible to pronounce.) What *is* important is your own personal discovery of the many attributes of God and facets of His character. The more you understand His names and their meanings, the more you learn about Him. And the more His character comes alive in your mind and in your life.

The name *Jehovah Chereb* means "the Lord, the sword." And it should give us great comfort in this unstable era to know God as our shield, our helper, and our glorious sword. The Lord promises that those who rise up against Him cannot stand in His presence. We don't have to lift a finger to bring about deliverance—simply trusting in God does the trick.

Because God can so easily remove our trials and troubles, we need to wait before we leap into action and take the fight into our own hands. Remember, no battle is too overwhelming, no addiction is too difficult, and no sin is too great for God to overcome. He has our back, and nothing can destroy us when we place our trust in Him.

Everyone born of God overcomes the world. This is the victory that has overcome the world, even our faith.

1 John 5:4 NIV

JEHOVAH TSABA

THE LORD OF HOSTS

THANK YOU

FOR SURROUNDING ALL AND BEING OVER ALL.

THANK YOU

FOR THE POWER OF YOUR NAME, WHICH

GIVES ME COURAGE

Whether it's a sports competition or a business proposal or a vacation plan, one thing holds true: If we aren't prepared, we aren't going to win. If we *are* prepared, there's a much better chance things will end up in our favor.

In the spiritual realm, when we're prepared, we can be guaranteed victory. That's because God has the power to defeat even our worst opponents. He is *Jehovah Tsaba*, the Lord of hosts—powerful, mighty, and sovereign. We often act cowardly in the face of trouble—especially if we're intimidated or frightened—but we have no need to feel anything but confidence if we have God on our side. Anything less is an affront to the Lord.

When we're feeling attacks coming in from every side, God surrounds us with His protection. Speaking the power of His name gives us courage and confidence, reminding us that with His strength there's nothing that cannot be overcome.

At times, others will attempt to give us faulty armor in the form of questionable advice, quick fixes, or instructions that are contrary to what God would have us do. That's when we need to stand strong and stay firm in trusting the Lord to work things out. He is always preparing us for the battles we will one day face. With God on our side, we can overcome any situation.

Our Redeemer, the LORD of hosts is His name, the Holy One of Israel.

Isaiah 47:4

.I NEED NOT FEAR.

ANYONE
OR ANYTHING
when the
GREATEST
OF WARRIORS
guides me.

JEHOVAH
GIBBOR MILCHAMAH

· THE LORD MIGHTY IN BATTLE ·

I give You thanks.

Have you ever tried to fix something on your own—when you had no clue what you were doing—and ended up making an even bigger mess? Often, you need to call in someone else to clean up that mess, which costs you even more time and money. If only you had called on the expert in the first place!

When we take spiritual battles into our own hands and forget to call on the expert, God, we can end up with a bona fide disaster zone. We need to remember His name *Jehovah Gibbor Milchamah*, the Lord mighty in battle, and call on that name in humility. Instead of piecing together how-to steps on our own or blindly fumbling for a solution, we should instead trust that God has the perfect plan for fixing our problem or issue.

Don't make the mistake of looking for big explosions or major fireworks when God is at work. Sometimes His efforts may seem invisible, but He's doing battle just the same. He's speaking to that person who has been spreading untruths about you. He's opening your coworker's eyes to the witness of your life for Christ. He's planting seeds of faith in that family member you thought would never experience the life-changing gift of salvation. Because God is capable of all things, we need to walk through each day in peace, living in trust. There's no need to fix it yourself when the expert is already at work in your life.

I will instruct you and teach you in the way which you should go; I will counsel you with My eye upon you.

Psalm 32:8

ALL-POWERFUL, ALL-KNOWING, & EVER READY TO STAND IN DEFENSE OF THOSE WHO FEAR YOU & TRUST IN YOU.

JEHOVAH MAGINNENU

THE LORD OUR DEFENSE

Finances. Work. Health. Family. Friendships. Church. Volunteering. We juggle so many commitments and activities, but sooner or later something is going to drop. We can keep our lives balanced on our own for only so long. Yet when we put our trust in the Lord, we don't have to worry about keeping it all together by ourselves. He has the power and the ability to give us what we need, just when we need it.

Sooner or later, something is going to crash down. Someone will treat us unfairly. We'll experience a major stumbling block. Our carefully laid plans will spin out of control. At these moments, God will rise up. He will enfold us in His presence and assure us of His love. And if we let Him, He will gladly take control and allow us to rest in Him.

In this world, all of us will encounter our share of unfairness, disappointment, jealously, resentment, and hurt, but God will be our defense—*Jehovah Maginnenu*. He will step in when our lives spiral out of control. He will be our champion and defender. That's why there's no need for us to justify or vindicate ourselves. Our task is simply—and thankfully—to live a life of faith and fruitfulness as we're reminded again and again of His truth.

Be strong and courageous, do not be afraid or tremble at them, for the LORD your God is the one who goes with you. He will not fail you or forsake you.

Deuteronomy 31:6

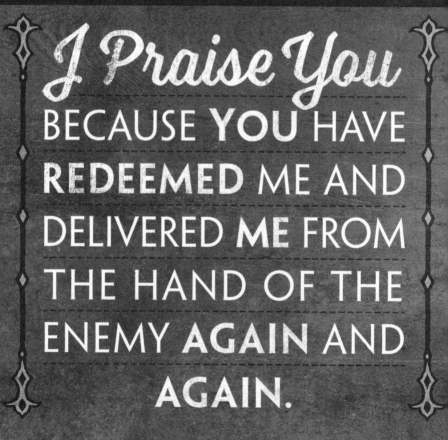

JEHOVAH GOELEKH

THE LORD YOUR REDEEMER

I Praise You BECAUSE **YOU** HAVE **REDEEMED** ME AND DELIVERED **ME** FROM THE HAND OF THE ENEMY **AGAIN** AND AGAIN.

When you attend a concert or a theater production, you don't usually get to see what's going on behind the scenes. You don't see the backstage crew or all the rehearsals leading up to the show or the countless hours of preparation that have gone into the event.

It's kind of like that with God's work in our lives. We tend to live in the moment, noticing only what's currently happening, failing to notice God working behind the scenes. We miss all the effort and planning He's put in, and we are unable to see Him intervening and redirecting on our behalf. Because of this, we lack understanding of all that God has rescued us from and the countless ways He has redeemed us. Still, He continues to work wonders in our lives.

God formed each of us for a purpose, and the best way to live out that purpose is to take refuge in His presence. He promises that none who take refuge in Him will be lost, and He will always redeem us day after day despite our lack of awareness and acknowledgment. He is *Jehovah Goelekh*, the Lord our Redeemer, our ever-present help in times of trouble. In His redeeming strength, He works daily wonders in our lives and hearts.

Thus says the LORD, your Redeemer, the Holy One of Israel, "I am the LORD your God, who teaches you to profit, who leads you in the way you should go."

Isaiah 48:17

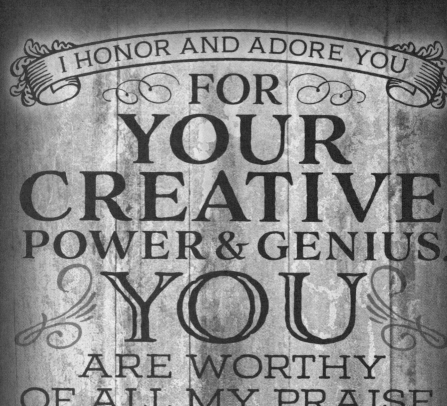

I HONOR AND ADORE YOU FOR **YOUR CREATIVE** POWER & GENIUS. *YOU* ARE WORTHY OF ALL MY PRAISE. **JEHOVAH ELOHIM** LORD GOD

Focusing on your personal relationship with the Lord during times of prayer and devotion is important, but don't forget that God created us as relational beings with a desire to connect with each other. Growing close to other believers is important too, so make time in your schedule for worship, fellowship, discussion, and study with others.

God created all of us, and His plan is for us to worship Him together. He's intimately involved in His creation. He cares about us as individuals, and He wants us to care for each other. God sees the beauty in all of His creation, and when we see the world as He sees it, we see the beauty in others—the skills, gifts, and talents He has placed in their lives. When we choose to see others from God's perspective, our view of the world changes. We're filled with appreciation and compassion, not jealously and comparison.

We're commanded to love others because of God's boundless love for us. And we need to open our hearts to receive love from others as a reflection of God's love for us. When life is getting complicated and confusing, keep those thoughts in mind: *Love God and love others*. When you live by this command, God will bring your life to full fruition.

Beloved, let us love one another, for love is from God; and everyone who loves is born of God and knows God.

1 John 4:7

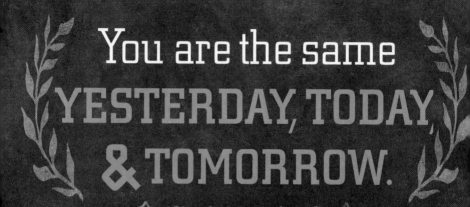

You are the same
YESTERDAY, TODAY,
& TOMORROW.

JEHOVAH
ELOHIM AB

THE LORD GOD OF
YOUR FOREFATHERS

I praise You for recording
Your connection with us
IN THE BIBLE.

We're so used to the lives of fictional characters through books and films and television that it's easy to forget that the characters in the Bible were real, actual people. If you grew up with Bible storybooks and Sunday school lessons, it can be hard to see the prophets and disciples as flesh-and-blood humans. And if we're unable to see them as relatable, it can be challenging to make the connections between what God has done for His people in the past and what He's doing for us today.

Yet God remains the same yesterday, today, and forever. He is *Jehovah Elohim Ab*, the Lord God of our forefathers, and all throughout history He has given every individual the opportunity and desire to know more about Him. We can achieve this by studying His Word and observing His interactions with those who came before us.

We are fortunate that God has paved the way for the destiny He has called us to walk in. He has provided us with every spiritual blessing, and His wisdom is available and accessible for all who choose to follow Him. When we open our eyes to our spiritual forefathers, we are given a glimpse into the heart of God's relationship with us. And we can praise Him for the good work He has done and will continue to do.

> **It is God who is at work in you, both to will and to work for His good pleasure.**
>
> Philippians 2:13

YOU ARE *Exalted* OVER THE NATIONS,

JEHOVAH EL ELYON
LORD GOD MOST HIGH

YOUR *Glory* ABOVE THE HEAVENS.

In a can-do, go-for-it world, it's easy to take control of your own life, start calling the shots, and forget that God is the one in charge. Especially when you find yourself stuck in a holding pattern and you're desperate for answers and action, you begin to make choices apart from God and can soon find yourself in a muddled mess.

When you're tempted to make a decision without consulting the Lord, remember His name *Jehovah El Elyon*—Lord God Most High. He is the one who sits on the throne. He is the one who can foresee where our actions and decisions will take us. And He is the one who best knows what we need.

God isn't simply in charge for the sake of being in control. He has a reason for every single thing He does, and our words and actions should reflect that knowledge of God's mighty power and position. When we truly believe that God rules over all and cares about all, we will begin to live in a manner that advances His will, passion, and agenda here on earth. So trust that He knows what He's doing. He is in control.

"My thoughts are not your thoughts, neither are your ways my ways," declares the LORD. "As the heavens are higher than the earth, so are my ways higher than your ways and my thoughts than your thoughts."

Isaiah 55:8-9 NIV

JEHOVAH EL EMETH

LORD GOD OF TRUTH

Let all the churches recognize the power of Your truth and teach truth always.

Have you ever had trouble figuring out the truth? Perhaps you're caught in the middle of an argument. One person gives you his side of the story. Then the other person shares her side. Both individuals insist they're telling the truth, but the stories don't match up. There are too many contradictions, too many opposite facts. Whom are you supposed to believe? Where can the truth be found?

Fortunately, we have one set of standards and one voice we can always count on to give us the absolute truth. God's truth is always perfectly pure and never brings any confusion. And He makes this truth clear and easy to grasp in His Word. All truth originates from the Lord, and that's why we need to place it in our hearts.

It's easy to undermine God's truth with worldly wisdom. It's tempting to twist the truth, factoring in our own experiences and ideas and thus changing it. But we need to take care not to do this. God has empowered us to discover His truth, and He doesn't make it difficult or impossible. He has given us wisdom, discernment, and a heart to know what is right.

When we choose to walk in the power of God's truth, we can make better life choices. We can help others. And we can trust that God's perspective is always superior to our own. When we apply His truth to our daily lives, we can rest in the comfort that comes from absolutely knowing what is true.

God is spirit, and his worshipers must worship in the Spirit and in truth.

John 4:24 NIV

JEHOVAH EL GEMUWAL

LORD GOD OF RECOMPENSE

YOU SEE WHEN I AM *Wronged*, & YOU CAN *Restore* WHAT I HAVE LOST.

When we feel as if we have no say in what's going on in our world, it's comforting to know that we serve a God who cares. He doesn't simply sit on a distant throne, removed from the pain that is so real and evident in this life due to sin and sin's influence. He's actively involved in each of our stories, drawing us closer to Him and revealing more and more of Himself to us.

At those moments when we're angry and fearful, we can always trust in God's great name. At those times when we're feeling lost, He finds us and encourages us to take refuge in His strength and might. He stands up for us when we've been wronged. He creates anew and restores what has been lost. And His care is always evident if we only look for it.

It can be easy to feel as if we're all alone, as if nobody is willing to take our side or hear our version of the story. But God always knows what happened, and He always sees the truth. He is a God who defends the oppressed, frees those in bondage, and restores what has been lost. There is mercy in His healing. Growth in His power. Peace in His knowing. In all things, God is our strength, and we need only to look to Him for comfort.

The LORD has been mindful of us; He will bless us.

Psalm 115:12

THANK YOU FOR

COMMANDING
YOUR ★ ARMIES

JEHOVAH
ELOHIM TSABA

LORD GOD OF HOSTS

TO ACT ON
MY BEHALF.

It's human nature to respond to a situation by trying to alter the circumstances or change other people. We quite naturally put ourselves at the center of the problem, and we base our responses on feelings and emotions. But attempting to operate from our own limited perspective and understanding doesn't usually work out well.

When we believe something is unfair, we should refrain from jumping to conclusions and taking matters into our own hands. Instead, we need to remember that God is always in control. He is *Jehovah Elohim Tsaba*, the Lord God of hosts, and He will always defend us—His precious children—and allow us to rest in His care.

Through our relationship with the Lord, His strength is made available to us. His forgiveness, grace, and mercy help right our wrongs. And when we choose to honor Him, He rewards us with His peace and His presence.

We don't have to come up with our own solutions. We are never left alone to fight our own battles. And we're never expected to retaliate when things aren't going our way. Even if we have been mistreated or overlooked, we need to resist the temptation to strike back or get even. We should keep the love of God in our hearts and look to Him to right any wrongs that have occurred in our lives and bring repentance to those who have wronged us.

> My presence shall go with you, and I will give you rest.
>
> Exodus 33:14

You rescue those in need

JEHOVAH
ELOHIM YESHUA
LORD GOD OF MY SALVATION

and bind up the brokenhearted

When we think of God as our salvation, it's tempting to imagine salvation as a one-time thing—Jesus dying on the cross for our sins and us accepting His gift of salvation. And while this is very important and true and the foundation of our relationship with Him, there's more to God's saving work than just a single act. When we call upon God as *Jehovah Elohim Yeshua*, the Lord God of our salvation, we're talking about not only an eternal salvation but also an ongoing salvation throughout our lives.

When we're tuned in to the God of our salvation, we're saved from making wrong choices and bad decisions and regrettable mistakes. Time and time again, His wisdom and guidance will protect us from worry, hurt, and regret.

That's not to say that everything will always go perfectly in our lives. But the God of our salvation is always there to offer us grace and goodness and to light our way. When we turn to the Lord God who saves us, He meets us where we're at, offering His faithful direction.

LORD, you are the God who saves me; day and night I cry out to you.

Psalm 88:1 NIV

Make me know Your presence

ELOHEI MIKKAROV

GOD WHO IS NEAR

so I can ever experience You in all I do.

Has this ever happened to you? You're floating on a calm lake—no wind to speak of and hardly any ripples. You close your eyes, lean your head back, and enjoy the warm sun. After just a few minutes, you open your eyes and are surprised to find that you've drifted farther than you thought you could. It's now going to take some effort to return to shore.

It's easy for us to drift away from God in our thoughts and in our hearts. We look away from the Lord and toward our own desires and our own needs, and before we know it, God seems far off in the distance. The good news is that we don't have to be anxious about returning to Him. He never abandons us or leaves us, and He is always closer than we imagine. He is *Elohei Mikkarov*, the God who is near, and He makes His presence known to us.

In times of distress, it may seem as if God has left you, but He is never the one who drifts away. We are the ones who drift. Emotions like fear, worry, anger, defensiveness, or confusion can cause us to feel distant from the Lord. Other people and negative situations can also draw us away. But God is always there to save us from experiencing unnecessary pain and regret. He will always guide us back to safe ground and lead us into a place of peace, comfort, and rest.

The LORD is near to all who call on him, to all who call on him in truth.

Psalm 145:18 NIV

THOUGH PEOPLE MAY DISAPPOINT ME, ELOHIM CHASDI

GOD OF LOVINGKINDNESS

YOUR GOODNESS NEVER FAILS ME.

I think everyone would agree that our world is in need of more love and more kindness. And while we should do our best to put others first and live for others, we also need to make God our focal point. That's because He is *Elohim Chasdi*, God of lovingkindness, and if we are going to have any hope of changing our world, it's going to be through the Lord.

The Bible tells us that God is compassionate and gracious, slow to anger and abounding in love. These aren't just admirable attributes—they're a recipe for how to live life in His image. And even if we do our utmost to live out these characteristics, we're still going to slip up. People are still going to disappoint us. And we're going to disappoint ourselves. But if we focus on His lovingkindness, we'll be inspired to show more love and more kindness, which can be contagious in a very good way.

In a world of anger and retaliation and negativity, it can be challenging to see where God is and understand what He's doing. But He is always operating in the midst of it all, filling us with the strength of His lovingkindness each day.

More love. More kindness. The Lord's lovingkindness endures forever, and when we turn to Him in faith, we'll be equipped to change our world.

You are a God of forgiveness, gracious and compassionate, slow to anger and abounding in lovingkindness; and You did not forsake them.

Nehemiah 9:17

ELOHIM BASHAMAYIM

GOD IN HEAVEN

You sit in
HEAVEN ABOVE
and on
EARTH BENEATH
You rule over all the nations.

Pull out a piece of paper and jot down a list of ten things you want right now. These could be material things—a car that works, new winter boots, a pint of ice cream. Or they could be more obscure things—appreciation for the work you do, better control of your temper, a positive attitude. It's easy to think of things we desire, but it's also important to get to the *reason* we long for these things.

Everything can be traced back to God, and that's why we need to make certain that our desires are in line with what God desires for us. He owns all. He knows all. He is over all. And for those reasons, we can trust Him with our hearts and our longings.

When we rely on *Elohim Bashamayim*, God in heaven, to meet our needs, He will go before us to open the doors we were unable to open on our own. He will direct us on a path we could not have discovered by ourselves. When we lift up our eyes and look to Him, we'll accept His desires as our desires and find lasting fulfillment.

Believe in God's promises, and He will shower you with His mercy and love. Devote yourself to discovering His will in your life, and you will be able to walk in the blessing and favor of His way forever.

Delight yourself in the LORD; and He will give you the desires of your heart.

Psalm 37:4

JEHOVAH HASHOPET

THE LORD, THE JUDGE

TRULY, YOU ARE ABLE TO RENDER JUSTICE ON MY BEHALF FAR BETTER THAN I EVER COULD.

When was the last time you threw yourself a pity party? Maybe it was when someone else took credit for the hard work you did. Or when you felt insulted. Perhaps you compared yourself to someone else and decided you fell short. Episodes of self-pity are fairly common, but they're destructive to our relationship with God and our relationships with others. They're also harmful to ourselves.

The best way to shut down a pity party is to stop looking inward and begin looking outward. Pray not just for yourself—also ask God to work in the lives of others. Don't search for what's wrong with you—focus on what's right with the Lord. When you put your confidence and your worth in Christ, you allow Him to judge situations and tip the scales of fairness. And you don't need to worry.

Remember, God is always holy and righteous in all He does. He has a heart of justice—a heart that is always faithful to the truth. He promises to be our champion, to defend us. But He also encourages us to step outside of ourselves and direct our energy toward doing His will and following His Word. He has the power to pull you away from your pity party, but you'll never find Him attending one. God has far greater things to accomplish. And He prefers that you join Him in His work and seek His kingdom.

Is anyone among you suffering? Then he must pray. Is anyone cheerful? He is to sing praises.

James 5:13

JEHOVAH HOSHIAH

O LORD, SAVE

YOU ALONE have the power to SAVE & I LOOK TO YOU FOR DIVINE INTERVENTION offering You the praise of my lips.

Help!" It's our first instinct when panic sets in and we realize we can't save ourselves. It should also be our first communication to God in times of need. Too often we attempt to come up with our own solutions or simply run away from the problem. But God will always rescue us when we call on His name.

We're used to second-guessing and questioning situations, but we always need to have total trust in God's intervention. He will never harm us. He will never lead us astray. We must open our eyes to see how He wishes to save us and take note of the steps that will lead us to freedom.

Ultimately, God saves us from our sins through His Son, Jesus Christ. And that's really the only saving that should matter. But because He is filled with compassion and mercy, the Lord also promises to bring blessing out of our misfortunes. He will bind and heal our broken hearts. And His loving grace will cover our wounds.

When we turn to God for help, we hand Him the mess that is our lives and allow Him to make everything new. When our first instinct is to call on His great and mighty name, He will save us and lead us in the way we should go.

Oh give thanks to the LORD, call upon His name; make known His deeds among the peoples.

1 Chronicles 16:8

YOUR PRESENCE EMPOWERS US

TO DEFEAT ANY ENEMY, OVERCOME ANY ✪✪ OBSTACLE, & SECURE ANY VICTORY.

✪✪✪✪✪✪✪✪✪✪✪

JEHOVAH IMMEKA

THE LORD IS WITH YOU

Loneliness. It's an increasingly common issue in our world. Even though we have the ability to be in constant communication with each other, it's also easy to feel isolated and apart. Text conversations just aren't the same thing as sitting down face-to-face with a friend. Spilling our guts online can often make us feel more alienated than accepted.

We need to strengthen our connection with God because He is the only one who will never leave or abandon us. We may sometimes feel alone, but if we live in communion with the Lord, we'll never be truly lonely. We can always approach Him and ask for His help and guidance.

Even in the silence, God is with us. Even when others have walked away, God never rejects our presence. With Him, we have a truly loyal companion who will always give us comfort and confidence and whatever we need in that moment. And beyond being a reassuring presence in our lives, God's strength and power can push us to greater heights. He can help us achieve the unexpected. And we can always have someone on whom to rely.

God's presence empowers us to defeat any enemy, overcome any obstacle, and secure any victory in our emotions, our finances, our bodies, our relationships, our families, or any other area of our lives. The wonderful gift of His presence means we will never truly be lonely and we will always have someone to turn to in times of need.

Surely I am with you always, to the very end of the age.

Matthew 28:20 NIV

I LIFT UP

MY TIRED
& WORN-OUT
HEART TO YOU

SAR
SHALOM

PRINCE OF PEACE

IN GRATITUDE
FOR YOUR GIFT
OF PEACE.

People are prone to worry. Tempted to doubt. In a stormy world where sides are chosen and tension reigns, God's peace can seem elusive. But it's not. We serve *Sar Shalom*, the prince of peace—the one who brings calm where there is chaos, stability where there is struggle.

When we choose God's peace, we are freed from doubt, bitterness, and regret. We can turn to Him for answers, comfort, and inspiration. He will show us new ways to interact with others and place words of healing and compassion in our hearts and mouths. The Lord knows whom He wants us to reach and how exactly He wants us to reach them. His guidance never fails.

If you're not sure where to start, begin with your words. Before you speak, ask yourself if these are the words the Lord would have you say. How will they make the other person feel? How will God feel? Will these words build a bridge or a wall? And are they an accurate representation of the heart of Jesus?

Peace comes when we abide in God's holy presence. That's why we need to let go of our own definition of peace and let God's peace reign in our lives. He alone can be the bridge between families, churches, communities, and nations. In His peace, there is salvation.

Make every effort to live in peace with everyone and to be holy; without holiness no one will see the LORD.

Hebrews 12:14 NIV

YOU TRULY SUPPLY
All My Needs
FROM YOUR
Abundant Riches
IN GLORY.

JEHOVAH
JIREH
THE LORD WILL PROVIDE

YOU HAVE NOT
LEFT ME WANTING.

You're uncertain of how you're going to pay your bills this month. The status of your relationship is up in the air. You've heard that job cuts are coming at work, and your position with the company is uncertain. When the basics of life are at stake—health, finances, shelter, food, family, employment—it's natural to feel terrified, as if you had nowhere to turn. That's when you need to call on *Jehovah Jireh*. This blessed name of God means "the Lord will provide," and it's a name filled with power and might.

When we feel fearful about our future, it's imperative that we turn to God and call on His name. Every good and perfect gift comes from Him, and there's no limit to the gifts and blessings He provides. Putting our faith in Him can sometimes be the only way to calm our fears and maintain a positive mindset.

It can be a hard lesson to learn, but trials here on earth strengthen our spiritual muscles and draw us closer to God. Through our struggles, He shows us firsthand how He provides air for our lungs to breathe and light for our eyes to see. He gives us exactly what we need to produce the greatest growth in us and the most far-reaching impact for His kingdom. And He always gives it in a spirit of love.

How much more will your Father who is in heaven give what is good to those who ask Him!

Matthew 7:11

JEHOVAH KANNA SHEMO

THE LORD WHOSE NAME IS JEALOUS

THANK YOU FOR  LOVING US SO MUCH THAT YOU ARE JEALOUS OF OUR AFFECTIONS.

Downtime. You might not have much of it, but when you do have a few free moments, what do you like to do? It's tempting to spend most of our unscheduled time entertaining or distracting ourselves. Watching movies or TV shows. Scrolling through our social media feed. Hitting the mall or the hardware store.

Take a realistic look at how you spend your days, and ask yourself, *How much time am I giving to the Lord?* God is described as *Jehovah Kanna Shemo*, the Lord whose name is jealous, but it's not because He becomes jealous in the way we sometimes do. He doesn't envy our snazzy wardrobe or wish for our fabulous job. No, He is jealous because He desires a relationship with us so much.

God deserves to be jealous because everything comes from Him. He sees the imbalance in our lives, and it grieves His heart when He observes us filling our time with anything but Him. When we could be diving into His Word or communing with Him in prayer, we're out giving our attention to the meaningless things of this world.

God loves us so much that He is jealous of our affections. When we put Him first in our lives—in our thoughts, actions, and desires—He will draw us closer and turn our hearts toward His.

You shall not worship any other god, for the LORD, whose name is Jealous, is a jealous God.

Exodus 34:14

JEHOVAH MACHSI

THE LORD MY REFUGE

YOU ARE MY FORTRESS, MY SHELTER, MY DWELLING PLACE, AND MY HOME.

We try 30-day diets, 21-day organizational plans, and 100-day fixes. We pour our heart and soul (and often our finances) into making a change, turning things around, moving in a new direction. And while goals and programs and motivation are all positive, doing things simply by ourselves can also result in frustration.

When we forget that we have access to God's power, we spend valuable time worrying, becoming fearful, dealing with anxiety, and trying to figure it all out on our own. If the plan doesn't work, we give up. Sometimes we want to just hide. Why bother even trying again if we're just going to fail?

We need to remember that we can always turn to God when we're feeling lost, lonely, or abandoned. He is our refuge when our plans aren't fruitful and life isn't falling into place like we'd been promised. When we're ready to give up, He will lift us up.

Keep setting goals. Continue to shoot for the moon. But don't let big-time failures or a lack of perfection let you down. God will always be there as our refuge, ready to shield us from the storms of life and guide us through trials and challenges. His isn't a 21-day plan, but rather a lifetime plan. And if we follow His way, we're guaranteed a successful outcome.

The name of the LORD is a strong tower; the righteous runs into it and is safe.

Proverbs 18:10

I am a CHILD and heir of the KING.

JEHOVAH MAGEN

THE LORD MY SHIELD

SHIELD me from ANYTHING that tries to get me to believe differently.

If you had access to an umbrella in the middle of a rainstorm, you'd use it, wouldn't you? Without the umbrella's protection, the rain would soak into your clothes and chill you. It would be silly to put such protection away during a downpour.

Sometimes, though, we refuse God's umbrella and neglect to call on His name *Jehovah Magen*, the Lord my shield. God is always ready to offer us protection and shelter from the storm, but when we get caught up in our own way of doing things, we run out from behind His shield. We're skeptical that He can help protect us, so we choose our own defenses—and those generally don't work very well.

It's important to remember that an umbrella doesn't cause the rain to stop. We still need to wait out the squall. Our feet might get a little wet, and the wind may be uncomfortable. But we still remain safe under the umbrella. It's a better option than folding up its protection and trying to outrun the dark clouds.

God promises to shield us from storms of all sorts—the enemy's attacks, personal struggles, difficult situations—and the shield of His name is always positioned correctly to defend us.

The LORD is my rock and my fortress and my deliverer, my God, my rock, in whom I take refuge; my shield and the horn of my salvation, my stronghold.

Psalm 18:2

YOU ARE MY STRENGTH WHEN I AM WEARY AND MY PROTECTION IN TIMES OF DISTRESS.

JEHOVAH MAUZZI

THE LORD MY FORTRESS

When we're terrified of the unknown and dreading the future, remember this: God *already knows what will happen to us.* He has paved the way. Nothing is a surprise to Him. If you stay connected to the Lord, you'll be traveling alongside someone who's already been there. Someone who won't get you lost. Someone who knows the way.

God is our fortress—*Jehovah Mauzzi*—and His fortress stands higher and longer than all fortresses on earth because He is eternal. The curious thing is that the closer we grow to God, the less we will wish to hide, fearful, behind His power and protection. Yes, we may always take refuge in Him, but we'll become emboldened. We'll seek out opportunities to spread the good news of His love and strength. We'll be inspired to contribute to His kingdom plan.

The story of God's great protection is a story of drawing all people close to His heart. And it's a story that can be told only through Him. As He directs our steps, we receive the wisdom to tell our world about His saving grace. The Lord will show us how to best reach others if we simply ask Him, "God, how can I make a difference today?" Through God, we are given boldness and opportunities to make a difference on earth for His kingdom so that all can have the opportunity to experience Him as their fortress.

The LORD is my rock and my fortress and my deliverer.

2 Samuel 22:2

FIND PEACE

and Hope

IN KNOWING YOU AS
RULER OVER ALL.

JEHOVAH
HA-MELECH

THE LORD, THE KING

Are you a decisive person? You might be one to quickly draw a conclusion, make up your mind, and take action. Or maybe you're the type that is careful to gather as much information as you can, weigh every option, and take your time making a decision. Each personality has its strengths and weaknesses. Each will have its victories and defeats. But we all have one thing in common—leaving the Lord out of the process, making decisions completely based on our own ideas, opinions, and values, will have negative consequences.

When God takes His rightful place as King of our hearts, we're released from the burden of self. We have the perfect resource to consult, receive advice from, and assist us in our decision making. Better than any self-improvement book or earthly mentor, the Lord showers us with hope, peace, and blessings on our journey to fulfilling our destiny.

In return for His love and guidance, we need to give Him the greatest praise, honor, and thanksgiving possible. As He humbles Himself to meet us in our struggles, doubts, and pain, we lift up Him and His glorious name—*Jehovah Ha-Melech*, the Lord, the King. And as we seek His presence, we will be able to have confidence that our choices are based on the Lord's way and will.

He is the radiance of His glory and the exact representation of His nature, and upholds all things by the word of His power.

Hebrews 1:3

Breathe into Me

AND LET YOUR COUNSEL TAKE ROOT DEEP WITHIN MY SOUL.

PELEH YO'ETZ

WONDERFUL COUNSELOR

There's no shame in seeing a counselor. School guidance counselors, marriage and family counselors, spiritual advisors… those who will help us reach our full potential can offer us valuable assistance in our journey through life. When we have the opportunity to make things better, to improve our relationships and our situations, we are wise to take advantage of those opportunities.

Life, though, can make us shortsighted. Often, we don't realize the need for outside help until the crisis hits. And then we're overwhelmed. That's why it's so important to learn to call on *Peleh Yo'etz*, God the Wonderful Counselor, because in Him we have access to the greatest counsel and the deepest wisdom we could ever imagine.

When we lack wisdom, we can go to God and trust that He will guide our thoughts, direct our steps, and show us the way through. He may do this by giving us deeper knowledge of His Word. He might direct us to professional help. However He chooses to work in our lives, He is always impartial and sincere. He always has our best interests—which are aligned with His kingdom interests—at heart. And His way will always bring blessing.

Major decisions and minor wonderings both should prompt us to dig into God's Word and seek His face. His ways are always pleasant, and His paths are always peaceful as He guides us in wisdom and understanding.

The Helper, the Holy Spirit, whom the Father will send in My name, He will teach you all things, and bring to your remembrance all that I said to you.

John 14:26

127

THANK YOU

for

coming to me

JEHOVAH
MEPHALTI

THE LORD MY DELIVERER

and whispering Your

promises
of deliverance.

Do you live in a land of what-ifs and could-have-beens? Do you spend time second-guessing your words and actions, wondering how things might have been different if only you'd made different choices? These thoughts are the tools of the enemy—and it's time for you to remove them from your life.

We lose so many valuable hours to fear and worry—hours that could be spent praising God, hearing His voice, and living out His plan for our lives. When anxiety creeps into our thoughts and causes us to doubt the holy work the Lord is doing in our lives, we need to turn our minds to *Jehovah Mephalti*, the Lord our deliverer. Instead of ignoring His deliverance in times of distress, we must embrace Him as our holy and powerful Redeemer.

Life is fragile, and God understands that. His Son, Jesus Christ, walked on this earth and experienced the human condition. He knows struggle. He knows despair. He knows agony. He knows what we're going through.

Emotional, physical, and financial attacks will take their toll on us. They can cause us to second-guess our situations and wonder what is to come. They threaten to rob us of joy, hope, and peace. But God is stronger than any struggle, more powerful than any problem. Peace comes when we trust in Him. And grace comes when we turn to Him in hope.

I will say to the LORD, "My refuge and my fortress, my God, in whom I trust!"

Psalm 91:2

Set me apart

to accomplish everything You have chosen for me to do.

JEHOVAH MEKADDISHKEM

THE LORD WHO SANCTIFIES YOU

And may I forever be kept close to You in

all I do.

When we see closed doors, it's easy to label them as setbacks. And open doors may appear as terrifying risks. Our human nature can be pessimistic and overly cautious, especially when we lose sight of the big picture. But God opens doors to provide us—His children—with opportunities, and He closes doors to protect us. Everything He does in our lives is for our good, and if we choose to remember this, we will not be afraid.

The holy God has set us apart—sanctified us—as His own. He keeps us in the shelter of His wings, and He sends us out to do His work and His will. It's imperative that we remember this. And that we fully understand that He chooses to do this in His own timing and in His own way. Our ideas and expectations may not match His, and that's why we need to stay in constant contact with Him.

When we spend our time and energy on things that distract us from our destiny, we're liable to encounter more closed doors. We tend to see these as missed opportunities, but God sees them as new directions. He has chosen us as His ambassadors here on earth, and He promises us that a life lived for Him will forever reflect His goodness and His glory.

Such were some of you; but you were washed, but you were sanctified, but you were justified in the name of the LORD Jesus Christ and in the Spirit of our God.

1 Corinthians 6:11

JEHOVAH METSUDHATHI

THE LORD MY HIGH TOWER

THANK YOU for providing a PLACE FOR ME to run to in my times of need.

We all have days when our thoughts and emotions are on overdrive. The smallest slight, the most innocent comment, the tiniest reaction…we're on alert to notice and magnify and read meaning into everything. Often, our responses are unwarranted and even downright silly. But that's what happens when we turn inward and start interpreting everything in light of our own faulty perceptions.

How comforting it is to know that we have somewhere to turn when the pressures and demands of life weigh us down. When we're overwhelmed with feelings and conflicts and difficulties, we *can* run away. We can turn to *Jehovah Metsudhathi*, the Lord our high tower, for reassurance and reevaluation. We can take our issues and insecurities to the Lord and ask Him to make sense of them for us. And we can gain strength to go on.

God promises never to abandon us to our own devices. He'll never turn us loose to confront the enemy on our own or make our way upstream through the craziness of life. During our most challenging days and seasons, He speaks to us, communicating His steadfast love and care. And He beckons us to come to Him, our high tower, and take refuge in a shelter that is indestructible, unbending, and unwavering in the storm. Before we respond to a trying individual or situation, we must make it our practice to first turn to the Lord.

Seek the LORD and His strength; seek His face continually.

1 Chronicles 16:11

JEHOVAH MOSHIEKH

THE LORD YOUR SAVIOR

YOU ARE VICTORIOUS OVER ALL, & YOU HAVE SAVED ME FROM ⦶⦶⦶ OPPRESSION.

If you're looking for a model of how to act and what to say in this world, look no further than the life of Jesus. And observe how He spent His time—caring for others while pointing the way to His Father.

Like Jesus, we need to share the good news of salvation. It's imperative in a lost and hurting world. When you open your heart to God's work in your life, you'll start seeing the countless doors He opens for sharing with others.

Just as God loved us before we even knew Him, we need to walk through our world with a mind-set to love others. So many times we don't know another person's story. We don't have the back-story to see what brought them to such a broken place. We only see their current choices and behaviors, and we forget that the Lord offers the gifts of salvation and sanctification to all—not just to those who are currently following Him.

If we're serious about glorifying God in all that we say and all that we do, we need to care for others. And we need to share the good news of salvation with them. We need to be bold with our words and bold with our love. Just like Jesus.

Be imitators of me, just as I also am of Christ.

1 Corinthians 11:1

JEHOVAH NISSI

THE LORD MY BANNER

YOU ARE STRONG AND MIGHTY AND ABLE TO DEFEAT ANY ENEMY.

★ ★ ★ ★ ★ ★ ★ ★ ★ ★

Worry only prolongs our stress. I know it. You know it. But as humans, we're never completely immune to being crippled by anxiety. And much of that anxiety is rooted in the past. We know we should leave it behind and press on to the future, but the past can be challenging to overcome.

Because of God's amazing power to overcome, He makes Himself known to us as *Jehovah Nissi*—the Lord our banner. If we choose to trust in Him, He will bless us with goodness, security, and hope for the future. He will stand with us in our thoughts and decisions, guiding us to the best possible options and solutions. He will move us forward and help us leave the regrets of the past in the past.

It's natural to turn inward to our own fears instead of turning to God, but we will always find ourselves in His reassuring presence if only we seek it. He is our banner when we're struggling with negative emotions, fractured relationships, failing health, or unfounded fear. And it is His will that we look to the future with hope and confidence, for He promises to give us the desires of our hearts as He leads us in His everlasting love.

Forgetting what lies behind and reaching forward to what lies ahead, I press on toward the goal for the prize of the upward call of God in Christ Jesus.

Philippians 3:13-14

You know the path I should take. *Show me* Your grace and Your goodness.

JEHOVAH ORI

THE LORD MY LIGHT

Light My Way.

Think of all the places where we rely on supplementary light. Lamps and overhead lights in our homes. Headlights, taillights, and fog lights on our vehicles. Flashlights or headlamps when we're running or walking at night or early in the morning. Basically, we need light whenever we need to find our way or accomplish something in the darkness.

The strongest light in our lives comes from the shining brightness of the Lord. His light is pure, holy, and strong, and it helps us navigate the shadows and dark places of this life. The curious thing about God's light, though, is that it will only direct us to what is good and to where He wishes us to go. If we choose to turn away from His brightness, we'll find ourselves stumbling through the shadows once again, wasting time and energy as we fruitlessly seek a negotiable path. We can become so consumed with our own darkness that we forget that God alone is our light and our salvation.

Though we can sometimes make a good guess, we can't always accurately foresee the consequences of our own choices—whether they're good or bad. When we reject the light that God offers, our vision is clouded and our judgment becomes suspect. We grope around in the darkness for guidance and answers, making small steps that often lead us away from His path of life.

So stay in His Word. Fix your eyes on Him, and He will light your way.

Your word is a lamp to my feet and a light to my path.

Psalm 119:105

JEHOVAH UZZI

THE LORD MY STRENGTH

WITH YOU

I can do all things because

YOU ARE MY STRENGTH.

There's a satisfying strength to weakness. Yes, that's right—sometimes the strongest thing you can do is to embrace your weakness, to admit that you don't have the power to make a difference on your own. In these situations, it's even okay to give up.

We're used to looking to our own abilities and efforts, but when we rely on ourselves too much, we forget about God and His strength and power. We applaud our victories, believing they're the results of our own dedication and determination, blind to the reality of God's hand orchestrating the entire process. We take the credit for ourselves when we should give the glory to God.

In actuality, we can accomplish nothing meaningful on our own. It's *Jehovah Uzzi*, the Lord our strength, who makes all things happen. And that's why we need to give praise where praise is due—to the Lord, on whom we should always rely.

Strength comes when we wait on God. Power is made evident when we hand our agenda over to Him and ask, "Please do Your work and Your will in my life." When we are at our weakest, that's when God is at His strongest. And at those moments we'll receive all we need to walk—and even run—in His truth to accomplish much for His kingdom.

My grace is sufficient for you, for my power is perfected in weakness.

2 Corinthians 12:9

With just one word,
YOU CAN
REMOVE SICKNESS,
REVERSE DISEASE, &
BRING
HEALING
IN THE CELLS OF
OUR BODIES.
JEHOVAH
ROPHE
THE LORD OUR HEALER

Doctors and dentists and dieticians all play primary roles in our world. We are grateful for these dedicated professionals—as well as others whose job it is to keep us healthy. But it's important to recognize that while physicians and medicine and a nutritious diet can heal us of many diseases and ailments, the ultimate power is in God's hands.

We need to trust in the Lord's power to renew our bodies, minds, and spirits. He has the ability to take away sickness, eradicate disease, and bring full and complete healing. Sometimes we may feel as if our prayers go unanswered, as if we or someone we love is forced to struggle needlessly, but our prayers never go unheard.

Whatever you're wrestling with right now, go to God in prayer. Ask Him to heal your heart where it has been gripped by bitterness. Plead with Him to heal your body where sickness has crept in. Request that He heal your doubt-filled soul. And beg Him to heal your words and your thoughts so you can share His love and compassion with others. In turn, God will work in your life and make whole that which is broken. The result may not be what you expected, but He always meets us in our time of distress. He treasures every one of us, and He will always heal us in a way that blesses us with life and abundance.

Lᴏʀᴅ my God, I called to you for help, and you healed me.

Psalm 30:2 NIV

Guide me with YOUR HAND & show me Your LOVING CARE.

JEHOVAH ROHI

THE LORD MY SHEPHERD

You shepherd me through life's path.

If you've been plagued by indecision or have found yourself second-guessing all your choices, consider this. You might be putting the pressure on yourself by fixating on your own life. When we're focused 100 percent on our own issues, we don't think anyone else can help us. And that's a problem.

It's easy to get caught up in seeing our lives as a laundry list of wants and needs, tasks to perform, and responsibilities to fulfill. And if we don't keep up and keep it together, the whole pile will come crashing down. Yet maybe that's what needs to happen. It might be the only way we learn to let go and allow God to lead. After all, He is *Jehovah Rohi*, the Lord our shepherd, and He promises to constantly look out for our well-being if we place our lives in His capable hands.

When we can't think for ourselves, God will think for us. When we're overanalyzing every decision, He reveals what truly matters. When we're worn out and overextended, He leads us to the place of deepest rest. We can't always see which way to turn or what choices to make, but the Lord will always be faithful in showing us the way. So ask Him to guide your steps and help you make decisions that bring honor and glory to Him. He is your shepherd.

He is our God, and we are the people of His pasture and the sheep of His hand.

Psalm 95:7

Thank You

FOR WHISPERING TO ME WHEN I'M IN DANGER, CONVICTING ME BEFORE I SIN, AND BEING THERE WHEN I NEED YOU.

RUACH HAKKODESH
HOLY SPIRIT

The changing of the seasons always brings renewed energy. When the snow melts and the earth warms, devoted gardeners till the soil and plant seeds, ready for a time of sun and warmth and growth. In the autumn, as the temperature dips and the nights bring frost, we pull out our scarves and hats and boots, stock up on firewood, and prepare to draw inward for the season.

When we've accepted the Lord into our lives, we are always being renewed and made ready for the coming season. Unlike the earthly seasons of the year—when we know exactly what to expect—spiritual seasons can be impossible to predict. We never know what God will have in store for us from one moment to the next. But with the power of the Holy Spirit, *Ruach Hakkodesh*, we will always be prepared to face challenges and accomplish great things.

The Holy Spirit is a guiding presence in our lives, a whispering voice in times of trouble, and a motivating nudge for us to step outside our comfort zone and begin to truly live for Jesus. The Spirit convicts us of sin and guides us in wisdom. And through the Holy Spirit, we are given a clean heart and a steadfast spirit. We are renewed and prepared and made ready for the season ahead— no matter what it holds.

If anyone is in Christ, he is a new creature; the old things passed away; behold, new things have come.

2 Corinthians 5:17

147

YOU SHOW YOURSELF STRONG; YOU ARE MY SHIELD, MY FORTRESS, JEHOVAH SALI THE LORD MY ROCK AND MY DELIVERER.

Most rocks don't tend to draw a lot of attention. They're not colorful or sparkly. They're often covered with moss or dirt. Sometimes you don't even realize a rock is there until you stub your toe or trip on it. There may not be anything flashy about a rock, but what would our earth be without majestic mountain peaks and raging rivers and colossal canyons? Rocks are the foundation of our earth. And *Jehovah Sali*, the Lord our rock, is the foundation of our lives.

As the rock upon which we build our lives, God delivers us from so many things. And while we tend to think of the ways He rescues us from major disasters, don't forget all the small ways He delivers us. He saves us from our own destructive thoughts. He can free us from worry and fear. He can rescue us from misinterpreting the words and actions of others. When we focus on His glorious names and attributes instead of obsessing over the pebble in our path, God delivers us.

When we step off the rock of His protection, we find that our footing is faulty. We slip and slide, trying to gain traction and find our way. That's why we must remain standing on the rock. Day in and day out, the Lord our rock is solid and unmovable. He remains our shield and fortress, protecting us from the darts of the enemy. We find safety and rest in the rock of His salvation.

Who is God, but the LORD? And who is a rock, except our God?

Psalm 18:31

JEHOVAH SHALOM

THE LORD OUR PEACE

YOU BRING PEACE TO MY HEART & SOUL WHEN I ABIDE IN YOUR PRESENCE.

Legitimate things can drain the joy from life. When you're confronted with family issues, financial difficulties, or health challenges, it's hard to find the brilliance and beauty in each day. Worry and fear hang like shadows over everything else, and we struggle to see anything beyond our own negative thoughts. That's the reality of living in this fallen world.

Through it all, we need to keep putting one foot in front of the other and following in the footsteps of God. When we commit to walking in His way, He will lead us through the treacherous terrain and usher us into a place of peace. It takes faith. It takes trust. And it includes an element of risk. But God always keeps His promises.

God promises us peace in His perfect plans. Though the future may be unknown and life may threaten to steal our joy, the Lord is faithful. He will never let us down. He will renew our bodies. Calm our thoughts. Heal our hearts. And clear our minds.

Jehovah Shalom, the Lord our peace, is who we should cling to when our minds are full of doubt and our future seems to lack hope. We simply need to ask, and He will show Himself to us and reveal to us the choices we need to make to enter into an even greater level of His peace.

The fruit of the Spirit is love, joy, peace, patience, kindness, goodness, faithfulness...

Galatians 5:22

YOU ARE HIGH
ABOVE THE HEAVENS

JEHOVAH
SHAMMAH
THE LORD IS THERE

AND YOU ARE HERE
WITH ME.

Have you ever tried to be two places at the same time? Maybe your body is present in a meeting at the office, but your mind is preoccupied with issues at home. Or you've spread yourself too thin and you don't feel as if you can give your absolute best to anything.

Try as we might, we can't be two places at once. And that's why it's so comforting to have *Jehovah Shammah*, the Lord who is there, working in our lives. God resides in our eternal home, but He also journeys with us through life on this earth. His glory surrounds the universe, but He also enfolds us with His love. He sees the big picture as well as the tiniest of details that even the most observant among us can miss.

When we know that God is always with us, we can take comfort that He will never leave us alone. He has gone before us and has prepared a place for us, but He's also with us to guide us there. Every moment, we are blessed with the comfort of His presence and the reassurance of His guidance.

When we're confused about where we should be and how we should be investing our time and energy, we need to remember that there's truly only one place that matters—being in the presence of the Lord. That's where we should be dwelling for now and for eternity.

When you pass through the waters, I will be with you; and through the rivers, they will not overflow you.

Isaiah 43:2

JEHOVAH TSIDKENU

THE LORD OUR RIGHTEOUSNESS

EVEN THOUGH YOU HAVE NEVER SINNED, YOU BECAME LIKE US SO WE COULD BECOME LIKE YOU.

Our hearts long to do the right thing. We intend to speak words of kindness to others. We vow to spend our time wisely. We determine to put the Lord first in our lives. But then the busyness of living gets in the way. We snap back at someone. We waste valuable minutes on social media. We promise we'll get to our devotional reading eventually. Our hearts are in the right place, but it's hard for us to pull it together.

When we're feeling insecure about our abilities and frustrated with our actions, we need to break things down and get to the heart of the matter. We need to place our focus on *Jehovah Tsidkenu,* the Lord our righteousness. Because He is perfect and holy, we don't have to strive to attain perfection and holiness in our own strength. All we need to do is acknowledge our own imperfection and lack of holiness and ask Him for His help.

The circumstances of life can harden even the most well-intentioned heart. Doubt can shred our confidence. The influence of others can have far-reaching effects on our own personal relationships. These are the moments when we must hold fast to our faith, calling on the Lord to lead us in His way of righteousness.

But God demonstrates His own love toward us, in that while we were yet sinners, Christ died for us.

Romans 5:8

You are the
humble King

IMMANUEL
GOD WITH US
who came to reveal
THE CHARACTER AND
HEART OF THE FATHER
to us all.

During the Christmas and Easter holiday seasons, we focus on the birth, life, and resurrection of Jesus. The songs we sing in church and the traditions we observe with our families place Christ at the forefront, and it's easy to reflect on the importance of God's work in our lives. Yet we must remember that God is *always* with us. He is Immanuel, which literally means "God with us."

The name Immanuel has incredible significance—as well as relevance to our lives today. God humbled Himself and came to earth in the form of man so we can understand what it truly means to walk with God. That's precisely what Jesus did—He walked with God. He walked with Him through all His struggles and trials on earth, and He walked with others. Never did there exist a more effective model of true love, sacrifice, and forgiveness.

Because God knows what it's like to be human, He understands how it feels to be hurt and alone and weak. Never distant and never removed, He is the source of our meaning, our purpose, and our life itself. God is with us, and His desire is that we experience His love more fully and intimately each day.

> I am convinced that neither death, nor life, nor angels, nor principalities, nor things present, nor things to come, nor powers, nor height, nor depth, nor any other created thing, will be able to separate us from the love of God, which is in Christ Jesus our LORD.
>
> Romans 8:38-39

YOUR HEART IS
FULL OF KINDNESS
AND GENTLENESS
TOWARD YOUR
PEOPLE.

GO'EL

KINSMAN REDEEMER

Have you ever thought that an important item was ruined beyond repair? Perhaps a favorite clothing item got covered with ink stains. Or your computer crashed, and you weren't sure if some important documents could ever be recovered. Worldwide, natural disasters have a way of wiping out the landscape so completely that we can't imagine things returning to their original state.

Sometimes our lives seem ruined beyond repair. We've made a series of bad choices. We've neglected to strengthen or even maintain relationships. We've lived completely in the moment with no regard for the future. When these things happen, we often end up feeling lost and unmoored. We can even spiral into despair and depression. *Now what?* we wonder.

God answers this cry of our heart with His name *Go'el*, the kinsman redeemer. When we think we're too far gone, He is always faithful to bring us back. He redeems the mess we've made of our lives when we reach out to Him and plead for His redeeming power in our lives. Though it may seem at the time as if things are beyond fixing, God can begin building back the shattered pieces of our lives and hearts. His patience and power will sustain us and transform us.

In Him we have redemption through His blood, the forgiveness of our trespasses, according to the riches of His grace.

Ephesians 1:7

HOLY, HOLY, HOLY IS THE *Lord of Hosts;* KADOSH THE HOLY ONE THE WHOLE EARTH IS FULL OF HIS GLORY.

You know the satisfaction that comes from a long-awaited cleaning of your house, garage, or yard? You want to share the fruit of your work with your family and friends and neighbors. You're excited for others to come see the difference. But that transformation pales in comparison to the difference God makes when He enters our lives and we become purified by His saving grace.

Through the death, burial, and resurrection of Jesus, we have been cleansed from all unrighteousness and made holy. His holiness transforms our thoughts, our words, and our actions. And we should be eager to run out and show the world the difference He has made.

The key to living a life set apart for God is to embrace the name of *Kadosh*, the Holy One. Instead of focusing on our past and present sins, along with the guilt and grief that can overwhelm us, we need to focus on His holiness. We must continue to give thanks for the work He has done—and is continuing to do—in our lives and hearts.

God's merciful love enables us to truly know Him and be accepted by Him. That should inspire us to honor Him in all that we say and do as we live a life set apart for Him.

Create in me a clean heart, O God, and renew a steadfast spirit within me.

Psalm 51:10

RUACH ELOHIM

SPIRIT OF GOD

Thank You

FOR LIVING IN ME AND
IMPARTING THE
WISDOM OF YOUR WORD
TO MY HEART.

We live in a world of comparisons. The lives of our friends and coworkers and acquaintances sometimes seem picture perfect. The gifts and blessings God has given to others may seem so much better than what He has given us. And we can feel as if we'll never measure up or be able to reach another person's level of accomplishment.

Emotions of envy and jealousy are warning signs that we are missing the whole point of life. It's not about us. It's about God. And it's about living our lives for others in order to point the way to the Lord. All glory belongs to God. All of it.

When we allow God to reign in our lives, He sets us free. We're free to live a life of kindness and faithfulness, of love and compassion. We're free to stop focusing on ourselves and start focusing on the Lord. We're free to put our hope and trust in Him. We're free to experience the fullness of His presence in our lives. Freedom comes when *Ruach Elohim*, the Spirit of God, reigns in our lives.

Even when we feel as if we're standing alone and wondering if anyone even cares, God stays close to us. He doesn't compare us to anyone else, and neither should we. He is the Spirit of the living God, and in Him we will put our trust.

The Spirit of God has made me, and the breath of the Almighty gives me life.

Job 33:4

You seek those
who are lost,

JEHOVAH
MALAKH

THE ANGEL
OF THE LORD

and to the lonely
You bring a
message of hope.

God has a history of seeking those who are lost and without direction. The Bible is filled with stories of people who have had encounters with *Jehovah Malakh*, the angel of the Lord, who brings messages of hope to those in need and communicates the need to rise up to those who must take action.

At some point, this refers to all of us. We all reach those points where we can't see the way forward. We all experience those setbacks when we're unsure of the next course of action. And that's where God will always seek us—in our darkest and deepest hour of pain, in the depths of our confusion and uncertainty.

God knows the path we are to take and the future He has planned for us, but He also knows that life is best lived as a day-by-day journey of walking with Him. If we saw only the ultimate goal at the end, we would miss everything along the way. And it's in those along-the-way moments that He teaches us and directs us and grows us in His image.

Listen for the messenger. He has a message of hope and encouragement and power—a message specifically designed for your individual journey and your walk with God.

The angel of the LORD appeared to him in a blazing fire from the midst of a bush; and he looked, and behold, the bush was burning with fire, yet the bush was not consumed.

Exodus 3:2

JEHOVAH TSEMACH

THE BRANCH OF THE LORD

MAY WE ADORN OURSELVES WITH THE BEAUTY OF YOUR NAME & REST IN THE ABUNDANCE OF YOUR FRUIT.

If you've spent time cultivating fruit trees, you know the importance of healthy branches. You need to prune them at the right time of year, provide the soil with sufficient water and nutrients to develop healthy growth, and cross your fingers that the plant doesn't sustain significant wind or weather damage. Only then can you hope to have a bountiful yield of delicious fruit.

Fortunately, we draw our life from the Branch that stays strong despite weather, soil conditions, or human care. When we adorn ourselves in the beauty of God's name, we can rest in the abundance of His fruit in our lives. Our task is to remain connected to the Branch—to spend time with the Lord in prayer, to hunger for His Word, to bask in His glory and praise His name.

When our hearts wander away from God and toward our own ideas and needs and desires, we risk breaking away from the Branch. When we step out from the shelter of His covering, our lives won't bear abundant fruit. That's why we need to stay close to the Lord, allowing Him to do a magnificent work in our lives and grow us in wisdom, righteousness, and love.

In that day the Branch of the LORD will be beautiful and glorious, and the fruit of the earth will be the pride and the adornment of the survivors of Israel.

Isaiah 4:2

YOU are LARGER than the UNIVERSE, but You also care deeply for me.

ESH OKLAH
CONSUMING FIRE

YOU are to be WORSHIPPED at ALL TIMES.

Have you ever witnessed the destruction wrought by a forest fire? It consumes everything in its path, jumping quickly over roads and bridges and even rivers. Now imagine a consuming fire that is larger than the universe, and you'll begin to get a small glimpse of the power of God.

We should have respect for God's overwhelming power, but we also need to remember that He is a highly personal God who cares deeply for us. And because of this, He is a God who deserves our praise and worship at all times. We shouldn't take Him lightly, but we also shouldn't be afraid to cry out to Him and to enter into a relationship with Him.

God's magnitude can be hard to reckon with, as can His attention to every detail of our lives. How can so mighty a being be so concerned with the seeming trivialities of our lives? It's because He cares about us so deeply. And that's why we need to allow His consuming fire to blaze strong in our hearts.

He is *Esh Oklah*, a consuming fire...but a fire filled with grace and patience and compassion. He draws us to Him, with the goal of us making Him first in our hearts, minds, and souls. And in the midst of the fire, He cultivates love in our hearts

Since we receive a kingdom which cannot be shaken, let us show gratitude, by which we may offer to God an acceptable service with reverence and awe; for our God is a consuming fire.

Hebrews 12:28-29

You are a

Father

to the fatherless

'AB

FATHER

and the

Defender

of those
in need.

I'm not sure what your situation is with your earthly father. Maybe you have a close relationship with him. Maybe he has passed away, and you miss him like crazy every day. Maybe he was not the best person in your life, and you've distanced yourself from his presence. Or maybe you never knew your earthy father at all.

Whoever your father is or was, he never was completely perfect. Maybe he abandoned you, or maybe he gave you his very best, but he could never be everything you ever needed because no human being is completely perfect. That's why it is such a blessing to have 'Ab—the name of God that simply means "father"—in our lives.

The Lord fills the gap and brings comfort and guidance to all who seek His face. And despite the fact that He has so many children, He knows each of us by name. He provides us with loving, gentle care while pushing us to new heights and giving us the confidence to take on this life with power and passion, facing the risks and thanking Him for the results.

It's not always easy being one of God's children. But there's no family more rewarding. No position more satisfying. We are blessed to live each day of our lives in the fullness of who God is and the peace that comes from trusting in Him as our Father.

O LORD, You are our Father, we are the clay, and You our potter; and all of us are the work of Your hand.

Isaiah 64:8

'OR GOYIM

A LIGHT TO THE NATIONS

RAISE UP A GENERATION WHO WILL PROCLAIM THAT YOU ARE THE LIGHT OF THE WORLD TO ALL NATIONS.

When everything else fades, the last thing you're left with is light. And even if the power goes out or darkness falls, we will always have the light of God. The Lord is 'Or Goyim, a light to the nations, and a light in each of our lives.

More than anything, He longs for us to fill our hearts and our souls with His light and then bring that light to others. For some of us, it will mean traveling to another part of the world and assimilating into an unknown culture. For others, our light will shine on the neighborhood block in the city where we grew up. One light is not more powerful than the other. Sharing the gospel has its challenges and rewards wherever you reside. The key is to be open to what God would have you do, where He would have you go, and what He would have you say.

So many people are lost in darkness because they have never heard of the Savior and the light He can bring to their lives. But His goodness and His grace are available to all who trust in Him. He redeems us and draws us into His light, for He has made His righteousness our own.

Let your light shine before others, that they may see your good deeds and glorify your Father in heaven.

Matthew 5:16 NIV

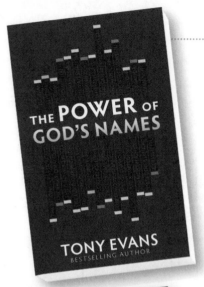

The Power of God's Names
Want to learn more about fourteen of the names of God you've met in this book? Discover what they reveal about God's nature and how you can apply those truths to your life. As you get to know the meaning behind God's names, His character will become real to you in life-changing ways.

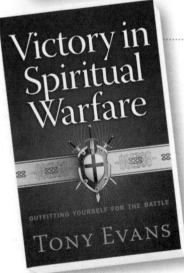

Victory in Spiritual Warfare
Dr. Evans demystifies spiritual warfare and empowers you with a life-changing truth: Every struggle you face in the physical realm has its root in the spiritual realm. With passion and practicality, Dr. Evans shows you how to live a transformed life in and through the power of Christ's victory.

by Tony Evans

Watch Your Mouth
Your most effective tool—for good or for evil—is in your mouth. Dr. Evans reveals life-changing, biblical insights into the power of the tongue and how your words can be used to bless others. Discover how to tame your tongue and use your mouth to speak life into the world around you.

Discover Your Destiny
Dr. Evans shows you the importance of finding your God-given purpose. He helps you discover and develop a custom-designed life that leads to the expansion of God›s kingdom. Embracing your personal assignment from God will lead to your deepest satisfaction, God's greatest glory, and the greatest benefit to others.

To learn more about
Harvest House books
or to read sample chapters,
visit our website:

www.HarvestHousePublishers.com

HARVEST HOUSE PUBLISHERS
EUGENE, OREGON